The Human Being in History

The Human Being in History

Freedom, Power, and Shared Ontological Meaning

H. Daniel Dei
Translated by James G. Colbert

LEXINGTON BOOKS
Lanham • Boulder • New York • Toronto • Oxford

LEXINGTON BOOKS

Published in the United States of America
by Lexington Books
An imprint of The Rowman & Littlefield Publishing Group, Inc.
4501 Forbes Boulevard, Suite 200, Lanham, Maryland 20706

PO Box 317
Oxford
OX2 9RU, UK

British Library Cataloguing in Publication Information Available

Library of Congress Cataloging-in-Publication Data

Dei, Hâector Daniel.
    The human being in history : freedom, power, and shared ontological
    meaning / H. Daniel Dei ; translated by James G. Colbert.
       p. cm.
    Includes bibliographical references and index.
    ISBN 0-7391-0685-6 (alk. paper)
    1. Philosophical anthropology. 2. Liberty. 3. Power (Philosophy) 4.
    Postmodernism. I. Colbert, James G., 1938- II. Title.

    BD450.D395 2003
    128—dc22   2003014081

Printed in the United States of America

♾™ The paper used in this publication meets the minimum requirements of American
National Standard for Information Sciences—Permanence of Paper for Printed Library
Materials, ANSI/NISO Z39.48–1992.

Contents

Foreword

Postmodernity is a reaction to modernity. In philosophy or in our historical consciousness it has taken different shapes. In analytical philosophy it has gone the way of language games, where use or the intention to dominate defines the meaning of terms. In social philosophy it has become a discourse behind a veil of ignorance, where rules of justice are set up purely in terms of maximizing individual self-interest, as if nothing had already happened rationally or historically to draw human beings together in mutual recognition of one another. In anthropology or in the philosophy of human existence it has opened the floodgates of deconstruction and dissolution of any human ambition to be something or to make something of oneself in the world, as if the failure of a Euro-centered modernity were the only paradigm for any future humanization.

Euro-centered modernity, which includes a North American version, not to mention a Japanese or an Asian Tiger version, has had its own narrative, its own discourse placing "man and his activities within a totalizing discourse," but the narrative does not always tell the entire story of humanization and dehumanization that has gone on in modern historical consciousness. To be sure, it tells the story of the human conquest of nature, industrialization, and the mobilization of technology at the service of human interests. But it does not tell the story of the loss of humanity in the process, the story of conquest over other human beings who have been excluded from the historical process, marginalized, if not totally eliminated, from what has made itself the center stage of world history. It hardly ever looks at the dehumanizing consequences of its conquests around the world, its colonialism, and its continuing rampage of cultural invasion through the juggernaut of multinational corporations trying to re-create the world in their own image and likeness.

The narrative of modernity, when told from the center, tends to overlook these dehumanizing consequences of its conquistatorial attitude. In fact, it shows little or no interest in what happens to human beings at the margins of conquest and exploitation, not to mention the explicit contempt for any semblance of humanity other than its own which one finds at times in the most sophisticated modern philosophies of history. From the margin, this dehumanization cannot be ignored and the problem of humanization comes once again to the fore in a new and more radical way after having been pushed off the center stage of modernity.

If we take postmodernity to be a metanarrative taking off from and taking issue with the narrative of modernity, we can see that it can take two forms, given the full story of modernity, one from the center and one from the margin. The postmodern view of modernity and of humanity in the making can be quite different at the margin than it is at the center. From the center it is possible to become critical of the modern shape historical humanization has taken, but those who have gained some advantage or comfort from the central power of modernity hesitate or stop short in this critique. They become complicit in the modern shape of consciousness as they cling to the historical standing they have gained in it. They have gained authority and power through this shape, and they are reluctant to slough it off completely in order to start anew completely in their historical consciousness. From the margin, one does not have such advantages and comforts to worry about. One has only one's liberation and humanization to think about. One is less prone to bad faith in raising anew the most critical question of historical humanization for everyone, not just the privileged few.

It is sometimes argued in the philosophy of liberation, which is the philosophy from the margin par excellence, that in a dehumanized world of oppressors and oppressed those who will be the true agents of humanization and liberation will come from the side of the oppressed and not from the side of the oppressor, from those who have experienced their dehumanization most profoundly and interiorly in communion with others rather than from those who have dehumanized them and in the process have dehumanized themselves. The oppressed are the ones who feel the problem of dehumanization most acutely and understand it most profoundly, especially when they understand what they have been deprived of as human beings.

Postmodernity has come to experience modernity as oppressive and dehumanizing. This is true for philosophy at the center of the modern world as well as at the periphery, or away from the centers of intellectual influence that are in collusion with the ruling economic powers. From the margin, however, the question arises as to whether the metanarrative of postmodernity at the center has truly transcended the narrative of modernity. Euro-centered postmodernity has been largely a passage from illusion to disillusionment, a self-conscious fall from utopia into dystopia, a sheer disintegration of the modern narrative with an affirmation of nothing for the new historical consciousness. It has remained a pendent to modernity, a determinate negation, to put it in Hegelian terms, without any positive result of its own, without any Aufhebung. Postmodernity at the margin cannot be satisfied with such negative results. It has too much at stake in the struggle for recognition in its own historical consciousness.

Postmodernity has become a matter of questioning and debate among Latin Americans, both in the shape it has taken at the heart of a Euro-centered narrative and the shape it has to take at the margin for a really new metanarrative that will free us from the old narrative of modernity. Dei tells us something of these debates as well as his own with an all too self-centered postmodernity that still wants to impose its own a priori rules for a discourse-ethic intent on preserving its advantage or its domination over the other. For postmodernity is a still too ethnic culture that persists in treating the narrative of other cultures as subsidiary in historical consciousness, as primitive or curious and perhaps even as interesting, but as of little or no consequence in the world historical process of humanization. Postmodernity's spirit can only trivialize the historical accomplishments of other societies whether by destroying them in the age of colonialism or undermining them through commercialization of everything in the age of neo-colonialism. None of this will do for a truly universal ethic of humanization in which nothing truly human is to be lost or discarded from historical consciousness.

In response to what he sees as shortcomings in the metanarrative of postmodernity on the northern axis of Europe and America, Dei offers the beginnings of what strives to be a really new narrative based on the existential originality of human being in history. It is a narrative in which philosophy is closely linked with the future prospects of the human project in history. In it philosophy is viewed, not just as an exercise in linguistic virtuosity verging on sophistry or as will to power, but as a search for meaning and truth about being human at the ever-present historical juncture where human being encounters another human being in mutual recognition and in the labor of humanizing the world. It is a philosophy, not just of information about how to overcome the other, but of communication with the other in which everyone is empowered to be fully human in a cultural space.

This is the kind of philosophy one is more likely to find at the margin than at the centers of power, among the oppressed rather than among the oppressors, a pedagogy of the oppressed coming from the wretched of the earth who understand better than anyone else that they still have much to gain in humanization. Dei makes no apologies for taking his stand at the margin. That is where he finds the metaphysical ground for affirming human existence in its properly ontological as well as historical dimension. Freedom has a constitutive dimension by reason of its very metaphysical marginality. It actualizes itself in one culture or another, which can veil freedom from itself, but which can also disclose it to itself in a communion with others. In other words, for Dei freedom in history is a sort of anthropophany, which he tries to justify in what he calls his anthropodicy, a view of history as justification of human existence for everyone able to enter into communion with others in search of meaning and justice.

Power is an important part of this view, but more in its internal and metaphysical dimension than in its natural propensity to dominate and lord it over others. It is a power to create one's own space in time, to make one's own place in history, to take one's own stand along with others, a freedom to be rather than just a freedom to have. But it is through the exercise of power in language and in the control of information as well as in the use of force that the promise of freedom can also be dissipated in a way that language games or deconstruction cannot reintegrate. For Dei this means that a proper anthropodicy cannot be complete without a positive sense of justice and law grounded in the metaphysical dignity and the ontological freedom and consistency of every human being. In other words, anthropodicy as viewed from the margin, where people have very little to defend besides their very being, requires a more substantive philosophy of law to go with its strong sense of community, something more than one finds in an abstract, loosely worded social contract dictated from on high that serves largely to maintain the status quo for those already in control behind the veil of ignorance they cast around themselves. In other words, it requires a conception of law based on the mutual recognition one finds in any community with a historical consciousness of its own.

This is a narrative for postmodernity at the turn of the twenty-first century that comes to us from the margin. Like any narrative it is framed from a particular place in history, from the margin as viewed only from the center or from a particular margin as viewed from other communities at the margin. This narrative has the flavor of Latin America, which has its own cultural mix of relations with the center as well as with the indigenous, the other who remains historically present in the consciousness of a mestizo transplanted from Europe to America. Nevertheless, the narrative is addressed to all human beings in their historical consciousness. It makes universal claims as an anthropodicy that should be of interest to any human being, especially those of us who find ourselves perhaps identifying more with the culture of the center than any at the margin as we turn into a new millennium. It is not a new millenarianism like that of modernity. It is a critique of all such millenarianisms, but one that does not stop at antimillenarianism. It is an approach to a new narrative that has echoes of a more ancient narrative when philosophy had to struggle against those who called themselves sophists, earlier technocrats of speech for its own sake. It is an approach to a real future for humanity in its historical consciousness. Coming from the margin, where the struggle for a better future often takes its purest form, unencumbered by a plethora of possessions, it may have a better chance of presenting the question of human being or of being human in its more universal world historical terms as a *pleroma* of human fulfillment, applicable in any culture and across all cultures.

As such, it should be of interest to us who are still more closely identified with an all too encumbered center. It is good to have this narrative translated into the language that has become largely that of the center. Hopefully, it will open up the philosophical discourse of this language to matters of more universal concern for an ever more historically conscious humanity.

Oliva Blanchette
Boston College

Chapter 1

The Historical Consciousness of Postmodernity: Reparation of a Dystopia

América aún,
cobriza, blanca, negra
abigarrada,
afollado sustento de la vida,
la del oro como el Sol
paciente
con memoria de futuro,
fortalecida en sufrimientos y en promesas,
te aguarda oh España a la mesa del Misterio
que brotará de luz la historia por venir
cuando los hombres de las máquinas
desembarquen desnudos en quimeras.

— H. Daniel Dei, *Memoria del futuro*[1]

I concluded my contribution to the debate *Postmodernism and Latin America*[2] by summing up the contemporary "condition of soul" with the popular expression *Dalle stelle alle stalle*. Returning to the question of postcolonialism, I would reverse the statement. Hopefully we will travel *dalle stalle alle stelle*, that is, go from the most ignoble to the most divine, from differences that keep us apart to those which enrich us, without getting rid of the story of the shadows that made some arrogant and blind and others rancorous and weak.

With Tzvetan Todorov[3] I believe that the genre of *exemplary history* teaches us that today, unfortunately, we are increasingly far from ourselves when we lose the *other* in our primary choice. This is the result of the lack of meaning in a planetary society ruled by the authority of the mass media. It turns the possibility of real communication among men into an object of manipulation, a monstrous device.

A formidably enticing challenge calls us to reflect. I would dare say it could be the object of a "new paideia" for the honest intellect, that is, *to exceed one's own thinking when thinking*. We should let the reasons of heart flow freely, as Pascal wanted, in order to see a more reasonable future. What has happened to the concept of universal, unidimensional, omnipotent reason when it remained at a particular position if not to enter into crisis, creeping into the darkness of cognitive onanism?

Certainly, whatever the reasons we state, the utopian plan of modernism turned out to be the dystopia now known as postmodernism. In the process, far from giving up its ability to take possession of and devour *other* possible worlds, the logic of instrumental reason intensified the efficiency of its discourse. It "performed" the great legitimating statements of modernism and emptied them of exemplary contents, creating at the same time a new great discourse. This discourse is the theoretical basis of the economic and sociopolitical practice which nowadays articulates ties among men. Still, it is refreshing that *thinking about the question postcolonialism* turns up in the discourse as the transcendental condition of the consciousness of "central societies"[4] both for their destiny with reference to the *other* and the possibility of being and existing from their own identity.

1. Discursive Context

Communication is only possible when there exists an encounter environment. An encounter environment must be built up without its component parts becoming things. It is a reality that cannot be delimited in any way. When one of the parties to this relation is defined, some of them begin to be manipulated. Then, there are not subject and object of communication but a reality environment which appears as encounter. When I think the *other* as an object, I find something before me, but "where there is a thing, there is another thing."[5] Instead of an encounter environment, I have built a domination medium with all its consequences.

That line of reasoning would have been unthinkable sixty years ago and remains so today concerning political, social, and economic practices. Perhaps, I should acknowledge that the ideal has encouraged the best minds of all time. But let us recognize that the practical endeavors of individuals and peoples tended to see only domination space outside themselves, a *means*—not an environment—for the growth of their own possibility and a means to find, through consumption of the *other*, the psychological safety that calmed the uncertainty of being. Few see that these strategies can always be changed and necessarily depend on the kind of freedom which makes them work.

Perhaps the most dramatic facet of the dystopian effect of the European civilizing utopia is the process of decolonization of Africa. The retreat of occidental "wise reason" revealed the fallacy of progressive accounts and commercial morality. Now, those "emptied spaces"—though not empty—do not inconvenience decision making by permanent members of the United Nations Security Council. *Our* wise reason leads itself to new genocide, while New York Stock Exchange strategists (and those in every market) celebrate high unemployment that secures investment profitability.[6]

Yet the extremely grave condition of African human rights does not seem to seriously affect the "humanitarian spirit" of governments in societies with their integrated history, despite centuries of discussion of how to gain real understanding of the *other* within. It seemingly repeats the symptoms of a congenital disease of the European spirit, the most efficient representatives of whose last stage has become the United States.

An early sample of the legitimating rhetoric of many subsequent European thinkers and writers is found in the Spanish humanist Hernán Pérez de Oliva in 1528. He declares that the purpose of Columbus's second trip was "to unite the world and give to those strange lands the form of our own." Professor J. H. Elliot comments: "Here, surely, is revealed that innate sense of superiority which has always been the worst enemy of understanding." [I would add of self-understanding as well.] "How can we expect a Europe so conscious of its own infallibility—of its unique status and position in God's providential design—even to make the effort to try to come to terms with a world other than its own? But this Europe was not the closed Europe of an 'age of ignorance.' Instead, it was Renaissance Europe—the Europe of 'the discovery of the world and of man.' . . . might we not expect a new kind of readiness to respond to fresh information and fresh stimuli from a newly-discovered world?"[7] That would be a reasonable conclusion if freedom of possession did not configure the sense of European existence, which nowadays is undergoing a decentering crisis of consciousness in the world of globalism.

Hopefully, though, thinking about postcolonialism gives a way to self-understanding precisely when it is considered according to the disposition of that *other's* vision which has remained hidden in the glare of one's own blindness. This show of courage is an invitation to think freely that needs to be kept safe from the shadows of astute rationality. Thus, it is advisable to find out whether the term "colonialism" is a *quantum* of self-consciousness that societies with integrated history have achieved in an effort to overcome that crisis of vital decentering or whether it is a new product of the great postmodern narrative.

It is not a question of dwelling on the proposal's intentionality, for a communication environment is where an encounter takes place. Transparency and ingenuousness in encounter never arise from ignorance or intellectualized discourse. On the contrary, they are possible only when *knowledge is a pain of soul.*[8] The fact is that the "text"[9] with which our conversation deals is still written in a language which forces speakers to follow the rules of colonialist or neo-colonialist speech. If the linguistic sequence between the prefix "post" and the term "colonialism" is linear and progressive, as I understand here, thinking about postcolonialism means to look at the reasons of the heart and to build the legitimacy of sense *with* and not *at the expense of others.* The task must begin by denying itself so as to exist in another text.

2. The Communicational Timeless "Tempo"[10]

How can we create a new discursive text, if encounter environments have been emptied of their historical condition? The formidable development of cybernetic and media techniques has crossed over geographical boundaries and has made our vision of the world planetary, just as the discovery of America challenged Europe's mental boundaries and altered existent social practices. In that virtual conquest of reason, can we positively assure that these technologies provide for the creation of communication environments favorable to going beyond our own thinking about reality? Is it possible that in a short term the explosion of navigators in cyberspace will implode into meeting environments? In fact, this is the condition that makes thought possible in the universe of mass media and interface technologies.

Won't we end by creating a narrative setting forth a paradigm for efficiency in social sciences as opposed to any hint of consideration of the attitudinal disposition of behavior? This formal and objective stance is paradoxical to say the least. In fact, the part of mankind that has the fortune of enjoying a certain quality of life is able to participate in the simultaneity of events. However, we should admit that their personal experience annoys us when we are drawn in, that is, when they exceed the entertainment and curiosity stage.

We are somehow impelled by the brevity of presences, involved in the visual collage and informative glitter, and in that contemporary dream world where every human event vanishes as a spectacle. I do not have the *other's* situation before me. For that, I need to stop before him and *let myself be questioned* within my own world, to change my attitudes, to reconsider my intentions, to feel pain in shame or enjoy acknowledgment. It is obvious that no questioning can communicate anything to me when the event is revealed before my consciousness as an endless succession of *video clips* that are another product for consumption.

That is why the discursive context in which we live can be characterized by the absence of communicational syntax due to an overdose of performative syntax. This diagnosis is supported by observation of certain phenomena which have been generalized in every field of human activity and guide opinions and decisions. Thus, the proposals of networks of communicational devices have approximated human contact to the *performative function.*[11] The performative value of statements increasingly requires a ruled text and a trained user for the contact. In this *interacting* pattern—the term is curiously precise—doubt, uncertainty, silence, and meditation are "performance" mistakes. If I am wrong, I am useless. If I think, I lose. If I am not in a position to be "performative," I am already ignored. The manifest ontology of the instrument—or better "device"—determines the *proper* extent of the vital time. To fit the rhythm of events, it is imperative to accelerate the response to the stimulus, to operate and remain at the speed of changes in every aspect of a relationship, even in the affective one.

Updating know-how is no longer the articulation of new senses and possibilities of self-fulfillment. It has become the requirement to show the latest in a market of varied, changing demands, of circumstantial utility, whether in industrial or intellectual work or the employment of everyday devices. The *teleprompter* might be the paradigm of a practice replacing spontaneity of genuine encounter. The underlying anthropology of this *"better acting"* ontology is the globalization of distances among countries and men.

Cyborg is a convenient model of performative perfection, because it can respond to the fictitious necessity of not evading the velocity of change. An aftershock of despised metaphysics is the possibility to aspire to "absolute personal experience" that turns man into a receptive-processor of multiple types of simultaneous sensorial stimulation. In this kind of discursive outline, any temporal or historical consciousness determines the dimension of abyss of a future that will separate men even more, the distance of lost progress where the "*majority*" has fallen further and further behind. There is no way of being-located-in-the-world in an ontological horizon marked by possession. Human freedom drowns irremediably in an illusory *tempo* of communicational timelessness, that is, in the rejection of any personal re-creation of the *other's* spiritual reality.

3. Simulation Logic

In the discovery of America a truly other self appears, hitherto unknown to European historical consciousness. It summoned a unitary vision of the planet even before Europeans were moved by astronomical discoveries.[12]

But real consciousness of this event, consciousness that may be expressed without operative conflicts, was not efficacious. There is no history without historical consciousness, Hegel said, giving another turn of the screw to the *hubris* of European legitimacy over other peoples. If I must accept that there is no history without conscious negativity, then, what has the dialectical movement of European thought been since the discovery of America? The negativity which marks the spirit for Hegel is the spirit's way of being. Hegel's term "negativity" indicates the power of maintaining oneself in *the other self*, which is also his definition of freedom. Are we talking about freedom of possession and its objective expression—execution as a social practice—in the power of control? If not, how can we explain the comprehensive vanishing of dialectical reason in his *Lectures on the Philosophy of Universal History*, where he is incapable of realizing that the Spirit's consciousness of itself might have found purification and transformation as the first fruits of America. As soon as philosophy is paralyzed by the possibility of being prophetic, its radical commitment to thought becomes dormant. It no longer accompanies every individual and people in their search for meaning, for opening the way of self-consciousness to their own improvement.

The opportunity America offered the spirit for Europe and humanity's freedom of being was lost, as lost to the very ideal or the Paradise Columbus thought he had found. Like a mirror of its own consciousness, the Paradise adventure revealed the true face of freedom of possession with which Europe fed Christendom, its waiting universe, a universe built on unsatisfied earthly miseries, hidden behind the legitimating folds of mercantile faith. Formerly hidden behind omnipotence and today discovered in the difficulty of choice, decentered consciousness uneasily faces a pretended common destiny, fragmented in its cultural background, pathetically skeptical about the historical result of its civilizing product.

Against this viewpoint, would it be enough if Europe leaves its origins to find itself as Heidegger suggests? Paul Ricoeur evaluates this alternative with invaluable intellectual honesty: "We must return to our Greek origin, to our Hebrew origin, to our Christian origin to be a valid interlocutor in the great debate of cultures; in order to have someone different before oneself, one must have a self."[13]

That judgment is helpful for our present purposes, and I want to consider it. It is easy to infer that the consciousness of the *other* self's singularity is what determines the genuine possibility of a communication environment and, thus, of an encounter with something different. "Singularity" here means that "self" which Ricoeur mentions; in our terms, it is the identity that gives us the possibility of being situated in freedom of being and, thus, being-able-to be with any *other self.* That identity, that "self," is what the French thinker calls the "ethical-mythical nucleus that forms the cultural background of a people," the images and symbols that are "the waking dream of a historical group."[14]

Certain questions present themselves at this point. Did not the elevation of this tradition give rise to that European consciousness of a guiding, ethnocentric destiny at the end of the Middle Ages, when Europe's vital horizon moved beyond the borders of the Mediterranean? Was it not precisely the singularity of the *other self* which the Greek, Roman, Hebrew, and Christian mind refused to admit, even contrary to its more clear-sighted thinkers? What behavioral logic has encouraged and encourages cooperation systems in countries of possible history when their needs come into conflict with political-economical interests of societies within integrated history?

We have a moral and material debt with Indo-America or, to use a Mexican expression, that retains the impact of the encounter, with the heirs of "pre-Cortesian" peoples. Thinking about the postcolonialism is thinking about the slowness of our consciousness to be responsible for the human virtues we have always praised and whose theoretical champions we are. It would not be difficult to validate historiographically the mutual simulation, the existential ambiguity of the antagonistic relationship between Europe and Europeanized America, of which I am, whether I like it or not, an involuntarily privileged exponent. Europe has been able to impose its conquering and colonial power. It has effectively absorbed *other* identity spaces, even with the help of many of us. Yet it has done so risking its own future splendidly, at the expense of finding in that human environment the possibility of recovering creatively as a cultural unit and projecting itself with authentic spiritual force for all humanity. Certainly, every profoundly decentered consciousness has resulted from the position of our freedom, never as a mere result of external phenomena. The exercise of that freedom of meaning in the world where we wish to live is our responsibility. Monsters we create with our fears for our immediate benefit inevitably, in the long run, devour us. Countries, like people, are ruled by the same logic.

4. Father Valverde's Tragedy

Inca Atahualpa was neither better nor worse than Pizarro. Moctezuma was neither superior nor inferior to Cortés. They knew that in war, one can lose or win. In their own way all were merciless toward real or potential enemies. Power of dominion was their model, and in their turn, they succumbed to it. On November 16, 1532, when he was tricked and imprisoned, the Inca said to Pizarro:

"The uses of war are to defeat and be defeated." A negotiation commenced, which was destined to extend the struggle of European identity. Like Cortés, Pizarro could have given a different turn to the history of humanity. But his mission was not to listen or to see, but, as Pérez de Oliva thought with grotesque simplicity, to convert everything strange into our form, that is, the form of a "oneself" (where he would never find himself unless he could *let himself* be interrogated by the *other*). Something else happened that day besides the conquest of an empire. Some accounts describe a ruse similar to that used by Cortés or by Agamemnon's Greeks on Troy. It was a small but decisive story in Fray Vicente Valverde's consciousness, a small but decisive story for the self-consciousness of Europe.

As stipulated, Atahualpa entered the walled square of Cajamarca with a large, unarmed escort to meet Pizarro. No Spaniard went to welcome him except the expedition chaplain Fray Valverde. Accompanied by an interpreter, he went ahead carrying a cross and his breviary. "Bowing to the Inca, Fray Vicente said he was a priest and made a brief exposition of the Christian mysteries. He explained that Popes had given the Kings of Spain the newly discovered lands. Lastly, he demanded that Atahualpa make himself tributary to the Emperor. Rejecting the proposal, the Inca asked: "Who has told you those things?" "This book," answered the Friar presenting his breviary. After examining the book, Atahualpa threw it to the ground. "The Gospels on the ground!" Father Valverde shouted. Immediately, all the soldiers on horseback with their leader entered the square. The Indians heard the loud noise of muskets for the first time. The sudden attack of the horses and the cruelty with which soldiers stabbed the Indians caused terrible confusion in the astonished escort.[15] "A short time later, once the conquerors had divided out the abundant gold and silver plunder and set aside the fifth part due the King to the liberation of the Inca, they put him on trial, and condemned him to die at the stake. After accepting baptism, the garrote was substituted as his mode of execution.

The tragedy of Father Valverde was that he prevented God from showing all his power before Atahualpa. Valverde's mind had already suppressed what his gesture pretended to do, let himself be questioned. The elegant god of the Holy Inquisition had definite purposes without awe. This was an intellectual god of moral operation, suited only to legitimate the mission.[16] A genuine kratophany at the request of the *other* would have meant that Valverde, Spain, and the whole of Europe did not enjoy divine favor exclusively. Furthermore, it would have been to confess the "faith in a god similar to Atahualpa's."[17] It might have been to *find oneself.*

A Quechuan drama still enacted in the altiplano represents precisely this moment.[18] Throwing down the breviary, Atahualpa confronts Valverde by showing that his god does not speak and, therefore, his pretensions cannot have consistence. The Friar's evidence and anger were what the propagandist Juan Ginés de Sepúlveda might have felt in his place. The empire and national interests of Spain were tumbling down. Besides, his chief, Pizarro, like Cortés or Almagro, "bore a deep faith in objects and things, like the ones that Europeans desired. They had inherited it from the Spanish court. But the latter played a fictitious role, because it needed objects, and as it could not manufacture them, it appealed to American gold, to acquire them in France or in Holland. Spain pretended to keep up with the century but was actually two years behind compared to the northern cities of Europe."[19]

At that moment of high historical density, Fray Vicente could stand neither the ambiguity of his ministry nor the impatient desires of his conquistador partners, nor the seduction of Atahualpa's magnificence and power. Such was the reason to suppress the Inca and everything he represented, especially as a possibility of self-conscious determination. The dystopia of modernity, still only inchoate in Spain, was on the move.

5. The Consumption of the *Other*

It will not be enough for Europe to banish itself to its own origins. Such banishment is a flight, an escape toward impotence to be-with-the-other. This type of banishment ratifies the presence of the dystopian side of omnipotence.

The tragedy of Father Valverde, indeed of Spain and Europe in modernity, is being closed to any kind of interrogation. To *banish* to origins is to be afraid of the question, not to want to listen. Jesus says to his Apostles, who, until that moment, had their own idea of his project: "'And you, who do you say I am?' Simon answered: 'You are the Christ, the Son of the living God'".[20] From that moment onwards, Simon became *Peter*, a self-conscious identity and an open destiny. What was the universal, the essential, and the *real* aspect of the mission manifested itself in the discovery of the *other's* singularity, in the act of *agreeing* to open new meaningful determinations in its *Weltanschauung*. To achieve that, Simon Peter had prepared his heart for the transformation that the question implied. The mystery of encounter is in this simple passage. When I am capable of accepting the difference—even the difference I am—I open the horizon of the possibilities of my identity, and I signify it again. For, the *other* is always a question to my freedom of being, an inquiry into the character of my destiny. That is the reason why the opportunity to think about postcolonialism may be the chance for the future European spirit to *learn to utter and then listen* for an answer to the question: "And you, who do you think I am?"

6. Rights to the Minority Spectacle

The Temple authorities suborned Judas to discover the characteristics of Jesus's power. From Moses they learned about the importance of intelligence-gathering prior to action.[21] They needed accurate information to achieve their objectives efficiently. Freedom of having and power of domination are phantasms of nothingness without spaces to clear. Information is power of *domination*. That is why the imperial will turns persons and peoples into useful information. Thus, social science, especially scientific anthropology, emerged exactly as instruments suited to satisfying the needs for intelligence about habits, lifestyles, and "capacities" of the *other*. What was alien would be thought and justified with the methodological elegance of modern civilization's operative rationality.

As data or signs of the temper and resistance of the *others*, we note that European political, socioeconomic conditions began to demand efficiency and "strategic" subtlety to shape barbarism. Consequently, metaphysical and ethical speculations on the principles of law, like those defended by Francisco de Vitoria and the School of Salamanca since the sixteenth century, had to be abandoned.

The Berlin Conference (1884-1885) consolidated the imaginary world of appropriation. It is difficult to deny that social-Darwinian rules of the game did not emerge from the core of that Reason in which Habermas still trusts. Philosophical and scientific thinking legitimated personal and national colonial territories in Africa under the advocacy of new, approving deities, gods able to institutionalize superiority without anger or culpability but with paternal strength. So anthropology achieved independent epistemological status and shared the ideal of positivism with the sciences of the age. Thenceforth it would not be necessary for Reason to be justified by appealing to the happiness of peoples[22] nor the civilizing character of Reason's purpose. Such motives are still reflected in instructions of the humanist Joseph-Marie Degèrando, member of the "Société des Observateurs de l'Homme," in "travel instructions" to French explorers in about 1800: "You are going South only as pacifists and friends. The wild Spanish adventurers take only destruction with them, and you will only spread benefits! They served the passions of some men, and you only wish the happiness of everyone, the glory of being helpful!"[23]

Science would accompany European and Western destiny by way of "prior decisions" and for more than two centuries would be condemned to conjure away inner chaos by imposing its legacy on any strange phenomena abroad. The "barbarian" would be "savages" and the "savages," "primitive." In due time what was savage would turn into a colony, dependent countries, developing countries, Third World or periphery, until at last the utopia of modernity would find only its own spaces to consume. Then, the anger of Father Valverde, Cortés, and Pizarro, confined in the labyrinth of European rationality, emerged with extraordinary vigor.

Power of domination is unlimited because it is the tragic illusion of Being. Baudrillard notwithstanding, the "work stoppage of events" is due to the revelation of nothingness in the possibilities of history, the disclosure of new awareness of reality, and the exigency to come to grips with a new dimension of existence, if we can see it in the pedagogical dimension that all tragedy has.

Nowadays that illusion of being, of "being somebody" or "something," is represented by spectacle culture, where drama and tragedy occur in the media—demiurge of life and death—rather than in real, daily life. We face the paradoxical alternative of winning the battle for our identity at the peak time of a program with high ratings. Man is the measure of a TV time and space or, a little more sophisticatedly, a page in the Internet. These are the new scenarios of a game of forces in which Western rationality is debated. In this quarter the *other*, the "good savage," has won space. However, local cultures, minorities, the strange, and above all the monstrous are consumer goods. After reaching planetary impunity, the penetration logic of postmodernity today flirts with the perverse and sinister elements that fed modern reason, in the dissociated folds of its legitimating discourse of freedom, progress, and civilizing order.

In this context, the right to a media spectacle might be included among human rights. Although the axial point of democratization has not been reached in this regard, the market has already conferred the nature of globalized, popular consumer goods, *commodities* of human communication and universal happiness to the supporting devices. These devices are able to efficiently replace at ever-decreasing cost old strategies based on domination of territorial extension. Through them human reality may flow without historicity, leaving no trail of temporal duration, diluted in new images without any engagement. Spectator contact is intensive and overfills human capacity of discrimination between virtuality and concrete situation, to the extent of relinquishing personal decisions to an authority which twenty-four hours a day exhibits its capacity to manage public and private life, producing senses of truth of any possible existence without muskets or lances. Not only do minorities have access to the spectacle, but they are protagonists. While their leading roles reconcile the diminished reality in which they live with larger history, with the great narrative of our time, at one moment, at another the mass media places erstwhile actors under the anesthetizing dream of having been. History thus turns into a complex of flashes of eternity.

7. Ethical Paradogmas

In living out our lives beyond any academic consideration, the ethical character of discourse lies in coherence with its effects. In this sphere there is no distinction between an ethic of conviction and an ethic of responsibility,[24] just as there is no subjective form of consciousness absolutely isolated from the incitement to historicity that human existence is. Either as human beings or as a landscape[25] *others* are always a necessary and present reality in the world we are in. The coherence or incoherence of the way we put our convictions into action is the effective measure of the values according to which we build our symbolic universe and the nature of the links established. We are responsible for the decisions that shape our lives. The history of mankind has arguably been a succession of dissociations between the reality we think we are and the reality we certainly are. In this tension of ambiguity, different legitimations that support the search for—and above all the imposition of—our identity, to "ensure" the truth of our beliefs, constitute the exorcism we perform against our own quasi-psychotic behavior. Whether as humble justifications for our acts or as substantial speculations, these legitimations are an unavoidable condition of living and the possibility to broaden our spiritual horizon. They can set a boundary closed to the plenitude of life itself, when they condition the creation of encounter environments if taken as paradogmas, that is, hypostases of reality in the texture of supposedly definitive positive knowledge.

The term "postmodern" captured world imagination during the 1980s. It allowed societies of integrated history in crisis to introduce a more efficient penetration technique than new muskets: the domination of the scientific-technological complex. In the 1990s the catchword "globalization"[26] summarized the postindustrialism-postmodernism pincers—a contradictory combination for some authors. "Globalization" fits the present socioeconomic paradogma and the misty values of the postmodern mind, the imperative of the staged political-cultural freedom. In this "systemic" context it is easy to situate and infer the real importance of individuals or minorities, or local cultures as Vattimo likes to call them. I have pointed out elsewhere that marginality "always expresses the circumstance of being inside a whole but not taking part in it."[27] In the language of globalization, this means that all peoples are involved in the project of mankind. The obstacle to involvement in the global village is that the speech of minorities is not regarded as a sign of lucidity but as a curious parable of the *divertimento* of the century. The parable stresses differences and turns paradigms of human development into paradogmas, ideological excuses to give an ethical disguise to the power of domination. The important thing is that with globalization no culture is "left out of history," as it could be maintained if the concept of marginality were applied in a restricted sense. Now, certain peoples must suffer the alienation of being in an irreversible world over whose configuration they have no control. Furthermore, we strip their future of every hope. Inclusion in globalization seems to have—in even harsher terms—the character of "cultural reservations" or "exotic zoos."

When, shortly after World War II, the German Medical Committee challenged ideological use of food by the Allies in Germany, it rendered obvious the status of being part of the whole. It claimed rights as a partner in the game of forces of Western rationality: "The medical body appeals to the universal conscience and asks that the alarming decline in the health of the German people be no longer allowed. At present, most people endure a diet that contains approximately one third of the minimum nutrition prescribed by international experts. . . . Prevailing chronic undernourishment has led to a noticeable drop of physical capacity and has not only reduced the efficiency of the German people, but has also seriously affected intellectual capacity as well as economic structure."[28]

How does "universal conscience" respond to human needs even more extreme than those defended by the German physicians, when those who speak for them are not part of the Western globalization process in economy, information, and culture? The 1996 United Nations Report on Human Development states that actual cooperation with the Program For the Benefit of the Less Advanced Countries (LAC) for the decade of 1990 was far below the initial commitment of the societies of integrated history, excepting Norway, Denmark, Sweden, the Netherlands, and Portugal. The commitment was even more adulterated in the concrete field of insertion and competition in trade, due to unfair or at least noncompetitive tariffs favorable to industrialized countries.[29] Although incomplete, the analysis provokes a comparison of behavior toward that *other* which rationality based on freedom of possession only sees as an object of submission. It also attempts to lead us to reflect in depth from perspectives that arise from examination of postcolonialism. While I am aware of no deliberate exclusionary mechanisms like food limitation as the twenty-first century opens, I do notice that we are dealing with an issue rooted in *our* conception of the world and that the living conditions we say we aspire to—steady, humane development, principled bioethics, recognition of cultures, and so on—present nowadays in international forum as well as in the packaging of household products, will only become effective if a substantial, new Copernican turn of Western rationality, self-consciousness, is possible.

8. The Reparation of a Dystopia or America's Daydream

Strategies of freedom are always reversible. Freedom to signify a world, that is to manage one's house and to take shelter in it, belongs to the essence of man. It is not a peculiar heritage of any nation. But the materials used to build the house depend on a prior attitude toward the feeling for life and death. Evidence of cultural diversity is also evidence of the multiplicity of possible answers to the issue of being in the world. "To be someone" against what is dictated by the wrath of the gods or natural forces is an alternative. Being someone by subsuming every uncertain space that resists our will to power is to install oneself in an ontology of devouring. It is to admit one is in a world ruled by relationships of submission. The process of devouring always has two directions. A metaphysics consistent with that ideal of mankind could not be thought in any other way. Just as it did in Greek thought, any presence crystallizes as a thing in the end, *pace* Heidegger. The dystopia of postmodernism has bared the crisis of European reasoning, again fragmented into the same domains that saw it appear. Possibly Hegel saw clearly that the journey of Spirit, weak and helpless when it was born, would find its definitive abode in the dialectical concretion of its ambitious destiny, at the expense of the aspirations to infinitude of the historical subjects. "Europe's greatest danger is weariness," concluded Edmund Husserl at the end of "Philosophy and the Crisis of European Humanity."[30] At that difficult time, men could not listen, because they had already turned to things. Like the conquistadors, the Western spirit has revealed its deep faith in objects and things. The gods no longer speak because their sphere has been desecrated and their devotees sacrificed on the altar of the Western mission, in the fire of the Spirit that has succeeded in consuming all of the *other*.

The issue of postcolonialism does not concern only societies of integrated history. Planetary man and globalized society are realities of which we Latin-Americans are aware. However, if this egalitarian uniformity of lifestyles only takes root in market language, the essence of the colonialist attitude will remain under new kinds of relationships and, perhaps, with names deified until the present.

To live awaiting superiority in order to be someone juxtaposes realization with an illusion of permanence. It is to fly over the barren land of antinomies, to grow in the pathology of inferiority. Colonialism or anticolonialism are attitudes that feed on failed encounters in a mutual search for vulnerable gaps. Rather than considering the "post" of colonialism, which might become a way of staying anchored in it, it would be better *to get ready to exceed one's own thoughts through thinking*. This means having the courage to discover a consciousness of history in the ashes of this history of objects we have constructed.

The discovery is made possible by the human condition of being, unavoidably and necessarily, *situated in a culture*. This means rejecting abstract universalization of human life by the hegemony of a reason common to all men, imaginable as a sleepless *cogito* that takes pleasure in industriously being God, provided that he is not disturbed by an insect.

Like any other the question of postcolonialism, asks about meaning. It is a turning point in establishing another awareness of history from a variety of possibilities characterized by our originary dealing with the human condition. The key to the challenge for our generation and its opportunity is *to learn to speak from silence*. The understanding of one's own identity in difference shows us the path to an encounter in that attitude, as Heidegger and his Japanese interlocutor[31] confessed. The symbolic universe of the *other* is the condition and hope of my dignity.

As in a dream dreamt by gods whom we have not allowed to speak because of our blindness, America accumulates the mystery of encounters of different men and cultures—descendants of pre-Columbian, European, Asian, and African inhabitants—united by the silent crossbreeding of *the hope of being-with-the-others* with dignity. This mystery is perhaps the wisdom of America; a seed soaked in an open and shared discourse, woven within the secret of the land to give shelter in weary times.

Notes

1. Fragment of the author's poem "Memoria de futuro," selected for publication in *Cuadernos del Encuentro (1492-1992)*, (Madrid: Asociación Prometeo de Poesía, 1992), on the occasion of the fifth centenary of the Discovery of America.

2. H . Daniel Dei, "La lógica del travestismo y metarrelato de la Postmodernidad," in *Postmodernidad y Postcolonialidad*, ed. A. de Toro and F. de Toro, Theory and Criticism and Literature Series (Frankfort: Klaus Dieter Vervuert, 1996), 155-176; see chapter 9 in the present work.

3. Tzvetan Todorov, *The Conquest of America: The Problem of the Other*, trans. Richard Howard (New York: Harper and Row, 1984).

4. Better, "societies with integrated history." This expression means that these societies already have or they are about to have their own history concerning culture and civilization. As Jean Baudrillard states (*The Illusion of the End*, trans. Chris Turner, Stanford, Calif.: Stanford University Press, 1994), 116 and passim, e.g. 70-71), they are societies which have reached a prostration point as opposed to what might be called "societies with a possible history," or one not yet integrated. See my criticism in chapter 9. My intention is to propose an alternative for all parties caught in the hypostasized relation of "central societies" versus "peripheral societies" or authority-obedience, where ideological connotations of such expressions dissolve progress. The phrase arose from an exchange of opinions with professor Raúl Oller ("La relación entre los poderes económico-políticos de finales del siglo XX y su proyección sobre América Latina," *The Japan Foundation Newsletter*, 1996). It helps signify that Europe as well as the United States can change the period of hysteresis they are in, that is of historical recurrence, if they find new possibilities of being by consciously recognizing the wrong place, the dystopia, to which their discourse led.

5. Martin Buber, *I and Thou*, trans. with prologue and notes by Walter Kaufmann (New York: Charles Scribner's Sons, 1970), 55. Alfonso López Quintás uses the expression "reality environment" or "field of reality" to point out that literary work must not be considered a mere object. The similar characterization of aesthetic object as "quasi subject" appears in Mikel Dufrenne, *The Phenomenology of Aesthetic Experience*, trans. Edward S. Casey, Albert A. Anderson, Willis Domingo, Leon Jacobson, (Evanston, Ill.: Northwestern University Press, 1973). Here, the concept has clear ontological-existential meaning and refers to the *topos* where, as we believe, every authentic communicative link has to arise.

6. The anecdote reveals financial Malthusianism about winning and losing. (We all lose in the long run.) It became evident when U.S. employment statistics were published in December 1996. Some experts held that employment rates should not increase in order to avoid inflation and continue financial euphoria. It would be interesting to fund research on the relationship between lack of creativity in long-term solutions and historical awareness or perspective of the occidental life paradigm.

7. J. H. Elliot, *The Olde World and the New (1492-1650)* (Cambridge: Cambridge University Press, 1970, 1990), 15. Elliot quotes *Historia de la invención de las Yndias* (Bogota: 1965) 53-54. For reflections on the theological legitimacy of that appropriation of worlds in the writing about Columbus, see Rafael Angel Herra, in "Descubrir o conquistar el Paraíso: Premodernidad, modernidad, postmodernidad," introduction to my *Poder y libertad*, 11-25. For a view on Columbus's personality, see Fredo Arias in the essays which have been published with Joel Barlow's 1787 work as *The Vision Of Columbus* (Mexico: F.A.H., 1992).

8. See Ecclesiastes 1:18.

9. My use of the term "text" basically coincides with that of Paul Ricoeur, *The Conflict of Interpretations: Essays in Hermeneutics*, ed. Don Ihde (Evanston: Northwestern University Press, 1974). For a view inspired in structuralism, see Eliseo Verón, *Conducta, Estructura y Comunicación* (Buenos Aires: Tiempo Contemporáneo, 1972). León Maturana's criticism of this position is found in "Sobre la comunicación social: Eliseo Verón," in J. C. Agulla, ed., *Ideologías políticas y ciencias sociales* (Buenos Aires: Academia de Ciencias, 1996).

10. I use this term as it is used in music. The composer suggests a rhythm for his piece, but it is the player's personality and general conditions which create his own rendition. In this way, the work appears in a meeting environment.

11. The expression is used in J. L. Austin's sense, *How to Do Things with Words*, passim, second edition, ed. J. O. Urmson and Marina Sbisà (Cambridge, Mass.: Harvard University Press, 1962. Notice that a possible equivalent is "better acting." Other equivalents to "performative" might be "executive" or "realizative".

12. Cf. Arturo García Astrada, "El descubrimiento de América y el hombre planetario," 71-79 in *Uno-Todo* (Buenos Aires: Ed. Almagesto, 1996).

13. Paul Ricoeur, "Civilization universelle et cultures nationales," in *Esprit*, October 1961. Cf. *Ética y Cultura* (Buenos Aires: Ed. Docencia, 1994) chapter 3, 43-56.

14. Paul Ricoeur, "Civilization universelle et cultures nationales," 52.

15. José Luis Busaniche, *Historia Argentina* (Buenos Aires: Solar/Hachette, 1976), 31. Cf. Horacio Urteaga, ed., *Los cronistas de la conquista* (Biblioteca de Cultura Peruana, 2), (Paris: Desclée de Brouwer, 1938).

16. This terrifying god was jealous and merciless toward the enemy or those who did not pay tribute to it. See, for instance, Deuteronomy 20:10-20.

17. Rodolfo Kusch, *América profunda* (Buenos Aires: Hachette, 1962), 106-111.

18. *Tragedia del fin de Atawallpa*, trans. Jesús Lara (Cochabamba: 1957). According to R. Kusch, *América profunda*, "This must be the most orthodox and oldest of the numerous versions among the altiplano Indians and mestizos," 106, note 1.

19. Kusch, *América profunda*, 149.

20. Matthew, 16: 15-16.

21. Numbers, 13: 17-20 gives a perfect example of military intelligence. At Yahweh's order, Moses sends his best men to explore the promised inheritance of Canaan. Compare to Cortés' strategy as shown by Tzvetan Todorov, *The Conquest of America*, 257 ff.

22. See especially Peter Worsley, *The Third World* (Chicago: University of Chicago Press, second edition, 1970). Cf. Claude Lévi-Strauss at the end of his Opening Anthropology Lecture, January 5, 1960, at the Collège de France (italics mine): ".nada sería más falso que considerar a la antropología como la última transformación del espíritu colonialista: una ideología vergonzante que le ofrecería una oportunidad de sobrevivir. Lo que llamamos Renacimiento fue, tanto para el colonialismo como para la antropología, un verdadero nacimiento. [. . .] Nuestra ciencia alcanzó la madurez el día en que *el hombre occidental comenzó a darse cuenta de que nunca llegaría a comprenderse a sí mismo mientras sobre la superficie de la Tierra una sola raza o un solo pueblo fuera tratado por él como un objeto.* Solamente entonces la antropología ha podido afirmarse como lo que realmente es: un esfuerzo—que renueva y *expía* el Renacimiento—por extender el humanismo a la medida de la humanidad." *Antropología Estructural*, trans. Eliseo Verón (Buenos Aires: Editorial Universitaria, 1968), XLVII-XLVIII.

23. "Consideraciones acerca de los varios métodos a seguir en la observación de los pueblos," in *La ciencia del hombre en el siglo XVIII*, introduction and selection of texts, by C. Bilbao (Buenos Aires: Centro Editor de América Latina, 1978), 120.

24. This example does not try to point out the theoretical aspect of this distinction but the political use of it as a deliberate overlegitimization of decisions to which many political leaders are accustomed and which shows the inconsistency between their principles and action.

25. By "landscape" I mean nature. Nature as substantial other, formed per se, does not exist positively for man. It can be presupposed but always as a world, as cultural order. For the groundwork of this approach, see chapter 3, "The Value of Freedom," of the present work. For further treatment, see my *La esperanza del sentido: El pensamiento metafísico del hombre*, chapter 5: "La naturaleza del paisaje" (Buenos Aires: Editorial Docencia), 4.

26. "Globalization and Culture," *The Japan Foundation Newsletter*, vol. 23, no. 3, December 1995, 1, by Professor Iyotani Toshio of Tokyo University of Foreign Studies, suggests a semantic correlation between the terms "postmodernism" and "globalization." I am responsible for the interpretation of these phenomena given in the text.

27. Cf. chapter 3 "The Value of Freedom," especially note 3.

28. H. Daniel Dei, E. E. Bevacqua, *El aborto de la libertad* (Buenos Aires: Ediciones Americanas, second edition, 1980), 51-52. Cf. René Masseyff, *El Hambre*, (Buenos Aires: Editorial Universitaria, 1972), 84.

29. Industrialized countries reduced their tariffs on products from the LDC by 25 percent But their tariffs on imports from other industrialized countries were reduced up to 40 percent. In this way advantages obtained by the LDC decreased remarkably." Sources: United Nations 1991 and UNCTAD 1995, *Informe sobre desarrollo humano* (Madrid: 1996), 119.

30. Edmund Husserl, "Philosophy and the Crisis of European Humanity," 269-299, in *The Crisis of European Science and Transcendental Phenomenology: An*

Introduction to Phenomenological Philosophy, trans. and intro. David Carr, (Evanston, Ill.: Northwestern University Press, 1970), 299. The lecture was delivered at the Vienna Cultural Society, May 7 and 10, 1935.

31. Martin Heidegger, "A Dialogue on Language," 1-57, 1982, especially closing part in *On the Way to Language*, trans. Peter D. Hertz (San Francisco: Harper and Row, 1971).

Chapter 2

The Sense of Philosophical Investigation

1. Clarity of the Obscure, Obscurity of the Clear

The quest for truth is another way of saying the search for man is always stamped with ambiguity. This ambiguity comes not from a conflict of logical principles but from the ambivalence of the finite and the infinite in the human mode of existence. Far from justifying skepticism, we think the ambiguity is symptomatic.

Indeed, a statement of Heraclitus approximates what it reveals to us: "The lord whose oracle is in Delphi neither speaks out nor conceals, but gives a sign."[1]

Thus, a simple sign, even a sign of contradiction, allows the direction of human endeavor to become more transparent and better illuminate man's path of reconciliation with himself than narrow conceptualization. Like the Tower of Babel, ambiguity manifests disconcerting difficulties in the product of freedom and imagination. It breaks the spell of operative reason's well-rounded, self-satisfied argumentation.

With a kind of voluptuous feeling of plenitude, ambiguity remits us to sense absent from (or underlying) clear and distinct concepts, and warns against attempting formal perfection through linguistic precision, which devours man's time, weaving veils over his decisive interrogatives.[2]

2. Encounter, Truth, and Human Being

Truth and man are in daily experience. They are path and goal. They lead the traveler in the measure in which he freely disposes himself for an encounter. There is no truth or knowledge when our openness is merely a door ajar, a psychological strongbox of understandings in the face of the uncertainty of inner disorientation and of social pressure on individual opinions.

The being seeks to unveil himself, open himself to himself and to others in plenitude and knowledge. This effort is to be—from himself and from others. In this two-sided unveiling he discovers himself situated in an essential reality, an ontologically consistent, meaningful horizon.

It would be in vain to seek necessary psychological security not rooted in effective awareness of experienced metaphysical insecurity. In that case man would assume a posture of being within the limits of socially permitted delirium, which doubtless would explode in anguish, desperation, or intolerance as soon as reality showed another face. In the abyss of radical situations metaphysical insecurity proclaims a structural dependence on the ground of every existence. Despite the silence of positive answers, this is independence and true liberation from the empirical chains that men forge for each other in daily life.

We hardly do more here than mention a remnant of freedom, less than adequately expressed. Propositional language crudely translates an attempt to objectify the possibilities each man must pursue with perturbed recollection, despite historical and social limitations, in the joy of discovery and the creative pang of personal shortcomings.

The truth of man is there: after the renunciation of the domination of the positive, of totalitarian knowledge of truth, and of the omnipotent presumption of knowledge.

We are human beings, and yet almost all that is essentially human is foreign to us. Knowledge of the world and the things man makes become deformed mirrors of his hurried desire to know himself. The cumulative growth of legitimating words tells the story of a thicket that devours every significant reference. The words end by drowning the silence of history itself.

These silences, occasionally pronounced both in community and individual life, constitute the word-meaning which men and peoples can hear in the solitary plenitude of the encounter. These silences neither say nor hide, but open perspectives, orient. These sporadic silences where the soul comes out are rich instants of ubiquitous communication with what is human in every time and place; they are the lasting wisdom that men have managed to harvest in their history, first fruits of the healing of freedom of spirit, that demand of each person the fruits of his vocation in *his personal time.*

That the truth and with it man may be present in us, may be effective participation in a realm of essential reality, it is necessary to listen to the silences of the word, to drench oneself in meaning borne by the simple audible articulation or the very language of silence.

3. The Calvary of Reason

In this ancient quest philosophy has a prominent place and finds its inner sense. Invested in human finite nature, its miseries and grandeur represent the best approximation to the *quid* of man. Man and philosophy are existence and mode of existence, means and motor, nourished by an immeasurable avidity of being and resolving themselves in plenitude. We hold that philosophy is essentially freedom, critical openness to consciousness and to meaningful totality. This critical movement of man's freedom makes use of reason in its aspiration to attain the serene justification of the principles of life itself. By "reason" we mean man's *proper* potency to open himself to knowledge of essences, that is, to what we have called "realm of meaningful totality."

Despite being no less substantive than man himself, philosophy does not express everything of man. Neither his action nor the results of his action entirely fulfill the profound aspirations which move the human existent to philosophize. Like John the Baptist, philosophy is a going-over, a meditation still profane, a lofty but worldly anticipation of the light, whose mission is to conduct man to the threshold of his own meaning and perish pathetically in the silence of learned ignorance.

Its responses affirm the aspirations of man to reveal himself to himself ontologically, secular epiphanies which proclaim in contradictory theses their profoundest need of religious communication.

This paradoxical dramatic dimension of philosophy is hidden to those who have made themselves comfortable in its bosom in a kind of intellectualized, practical realism, at bottom torn from the truly positive experience of living.[3] Just as they lose man in a complicated circumlocution of ethical formalisms, so also the sense and the task of philosophizing withdraw from life and desperately agonize in the scientistic fallacy. Against this background, philosophy still attains legitimation in its will to communicate;[4] it is accused of incapacity when it heroically rends itself amid the shadows of finitude in order to account for the measure of what we are; when it does not entirely resign itself to the narcissistic sedatives of "linguistic games" or the secular profits of even the most subtle totalizing explanations like parascientific ideologies. These are certainly efficacious in contests of opinion but insubstantial at the moment of decisive truths of existence.

If philosophy has a contemporary mission distinct from justifying its existence by desperately clawing for a niche in the leftovers of particular sciences as a reward for old services, the mission is to boldly carry on in the best Socratic spirit. Then it will rise from its roots and honor its history as implacable critical consciousness. Then it will viscerally take charge of permanent, open questions of human existence and being in the world.

4. The Epiphany of Reason

The acceptance of a manner of philosophizing, and the explicit or implicit choice of a definition of philosophy, compromises the task and its very meaning, just as the internalized values which sustain man condition his conduct overall. If these affirmations are pondered, it will be seen that we do not appeal to a mere essentialist device which puts the cart before the horse to explain the latter.

However they may try, human beings cannot be foreign to themselves. Nor have the series of systematizing endeavors and intellectual distinctions in the history of philosophy been able to frustrate the existential outburst which gave philosophy its passport in the universe of human possibilities. Hence philosophy cannot consist only in dissolving incorrect linguistic confusions or category mistakes, even if committed during the process of excessive intellectualization of the existential, ontological aspirations of man.

As analytic philosophy claims, philosophy does have a clarifying role; not precisely to abort metaphysical interrogatives, but to level hidden obstacles to self-knowledge, in other words, to clear the path of freedom. So-called philosophical problems do not dissolve in virtue of more or less clear reason nor are they neutralized by the adoption of one or another system of thought. They respond to the human need for meaning (rather than for explanation) and appear under other modes, beyond any utterance about a lack of presuppositions or the affirmation of positive knowledge alternative to philosophy, which in any case smacks of tacit rationality.

It is not necessary to repress theoretical philosophical activity to favor some praxis. The latter's incapacity to resolve itself meaningfully for man further veils previous thematization of values which re-signify his ontological necessity and mortgage the possibilities of his freedom. Both postures are theoretical. In either one we find the project of legitimating a possible mode of existence and the necessity of universalizing and even grounding it in the "psychological power" which accompanies an established rationality, in this case, that of science. On the level of collective action this has been known as ideology.[5]

What, then, is philosophy which attracts diverse enmities and requires so many corrections? Behind every argument is there a will to legitimate an interpretation of man? Here again we find the essentialist circle. Perhaps independently of intellectualization, philosophy shows us that it is not juxtaposed to man's vital interests but maintains an essential correspondence with them, despite the way philosophers and men generally have bungled and go on bungling their potentiality to be.

How should we sum up this discipline which brings together the contradictions of man himself? From our viewpoint, such a characterization of philosophy can in no way be disconnected from the historical vicissitudes which are consubstantial to it. Indeed they constitute the very memory of reason which even in identity fights to be faithful to the weave of interpositions with reality in order to achieve a habitable world of its own. We noted that while philosophy is essential to man, it does not express him completely. Rather than a defect, this is a signal which helps us immunize ourselves against absolutisms with which we habitually configure our most vital decisions and instruments with which we claim to legitimate them. An approximative definition of philosophy ought to contain the portion of humility which philosophy's name implies, and of freedom which every investigation about meaning demands. It cannot be mere science in the acceptation of pure, presuppositionless theory, nor particular positive knowledge at the service of a determined project of rationality. Philosophy is the highest expression of reason, lived as an attitude, a path, a way of life, and, also, a particular encounter with knowing.

5. Question and Problem

Our proposal can be better explained by elaborating upon the infrequent distinction between problem and question. This distinction is fundamental in many ways. It is an important element in our general conception. Used critically and rigorously, the two notions allow us to dissolve and neutralize many if not all objections about the uselessness of philosophical answers; they point toward the sense of investigation in philosophy and help us transcend the historical conversation of deaf interlocutors about undesired consequences of the philosophical task, which tend to be regarded as inherent properties of philosophizing.

Bergson affirmed:

> philosophy is a jig-saw puzzle where the problem is to construct with the pieces that society gives us the design it is unwilling to show. . . . But the truth is that in philosophy and even elsewhere it is a question of *finding* the problem and consequently of *positing* it, even more than of solving it. For a speculative problem is solved as soon as it is properly stated. By that I mean that its solution exists then, although it may remain hidden, and so to speak covered up: the only thing left is to *un*cover it. But stating the problem is not simply uncovering, it is inventing. Discovery, or uncovering, has to do with what already exists actually or virtually; it was therefore certain to happen sooner or later. Invention gives being to what did not exist; it might never have happened. Already in mathematics and still more in metaphysics, the effort of invention consists most often in raising the problem, in creating the terms in which it will be stated. The stating and solving of the problem are here very close to being equivalent; the truly great problems are set forth only when they are solved.[6]

In reality, what is settled in the truly great problems is the disposition, the spiritual attitude that encourages us to discover a possible meaningful horizon, but strictly, we should not speak of "solution" in this case. The great problems of which Bergson speaks in this important passage are questions, which is to say, interrogatives that in the very act of being formulated open perspectives of meaning for the interrogator.

Questions illuminate a path toward the comprehension of the world, orient us in investigation and the search for truth, even if by nature they are not positively resolved after the fashion of scientific answers. That which scientific answers clarify is mediated by information and instruments. In a problem, what confronts us is an unknown to be settled only by a datum we lack, which may always appear with time. Therefore, we expect solutions from science, the remedy of present lack of information. Hence also, we are confident of its efficacy, although the solution may be far away in time. But it is fallacious to argue, as positivism has notoriously done in our culture, that *all* questions can and will be resolved by science in a near or distant future.

In our time men believe that the problematic character of human affairs is uniform, because they can apply given methods and procedures to resolve problems in every sphere of social activity. The impression of power and infinite ability to manipulate due to the organization of information supports a temptation to the absolute, to completion, and security. Succumbing to that temptation, we frivolously cut short radical situations in life suppressing their differences. We seek and expect answers that are similar and of the same type for interrogatives whose ontological weight exceeds the positive results we can obtain by the resolution of factual problems, whose only impact is in circumstantial operational success concerning a problem.

A problem, or rather as Bergson has told us,[7] correctly posing a problem, implies the possibility of its solution if we can satisfy its demand for information within the framework of an appropriate methodology. This is normally what happens in science and in the resolution of daily affairs. In philosophy there are questions, which despite being well formulated, will not even be solved with the accumulation of more information or the employment of pertinent procedures of particular science. Whenever solutions have been found in the history of thought, they were not to properly philosophical "problems." Hence, they came to form part of a special science. Inversely, when scientists pose ultimate interrogatives such as what is life, what is the origin of the universe, or what is time, they know that they enter the domain of questions which transcend the limits of the objectives of scientific knowledge, and that whatever attitude they adopt in this respect will require an appeal to extratextual elements.

With the progress of science, philosophical questions accentuate their intensive nature. By contrast, requirements of problems accelerate an accumulative or extensive dimension of knowledge. Alienation of meaning arrives when we put our hopes in the positive solution of knowledge at the cost of open interrogatives about questions; stimulated by the enjoyment of freedom won in each interrogative, questions open the doors to higher grades of knowledge. In these acts of interrogation man liberates himself from the leveling positivization of knowledge of understanding and becomes capable of letting reason go to new existentially meaningful dimensions, thanks to the superior disposition of awareness that each interrogative discovers.

Therefore, philosophy is a preparatory path for wisdom, a singular and excellent witness to the possibilities of human reason. Not that philosophy is wisdom in itself nor is the philosopher necessarily wise. Paradoxically, like men in general, the philosophers can come to be wise when they understand the difference and do not exhaust the way. Wisdom is not a terminus of knowledge, but a disposition of the soul in the presence of truth, exempt from the intellectual possessiveness of the truth. The humble and profound lived experience of questions is its gateway.

6. Encounter with Man

In the course of its history the consubstantiality of philosophical questions with ultimate concerns of man has allowed that our discipline be exalted in rank with regard to the knowledge of science. Conversely, its weaknesses of finitude and impotence to effectively specify propositions capable of transforming the world have also been stressed. If the understanding opposes these emphases, on a different level, reason speaks to us about the unity between the human and the philosophical calling.

Let us return to Heraclitus and quote another fragment to complement the fragment reproduced earlier: "(One must remember also) the man who forgets which way the road leads."[8]

The two fragments express an attitude of reason lived as a path, a way of life, and peculiar encounter with knowledge above the ambivalent determination of the tension between the finite and infinite of our aspiration.

In Western thought the paradigm of this reason is the incorruptible gadfly of the conscience of Athens. We need to emulate and multiply his witness tirelessly today. Through it philosophy was smitten with fidelity to the fire of the gods and the heroic love for man. Mediator therefore between the sacred and the profane, philosophy alternatively suffers from a divine lethargy that has enveloped its existence and from the zeal for a vigilant love; philosophy is attentive to clarity of life nourished by hope for truth starting from the pain of the limitations of a mission that will be achieved beyond it.

The meaning of philosophical investigation is, thus, to accompany man in the passage to consciousness of his dignity.

Notes

1. G. S. Kirk and J. E. Raven, *The Presocratic Philosophers* (New York and London: Cambridge University Press, 1971), 211, no. 247.

2. Obviously, we use "ambiguity" here in a way that exceeds its usual meaning in logic. Rather, we emphatically appeal to its existential, ontological implications.

3. Here we are thinking about contemporary neopositivist and specifically analytic approaches, that, to our mind, desperately seek a kind of "ametaphysical empirical ground" of questions which *in fact* demand metaphysical consideration.

4. Cf. among other works, Karl Jaspers, *Philosophy*, trans. E. B. Ashton (Chicago: University of Chicago Press, 1970), vol. 2, part I, especially 3. See also "On Ciphers" part IV, in *Philosophical Faith and Revelation*, trans. E. B. Ashton (New York: Harper and Row, 1967), 92-127. Also Rodolfo M. Agoglia, "La filosofía como 'sabiduría del amor,'" in *Revista de Filosofía*, no. 17 (La Plata: Facultad de Humanidades, 1966).

5. Jürgen Habermas, "Conocimiento e interés," in *Ciencia y Técnica como ideología*, trans. Manuel Garrido, (Madrid, Tecnos, 1986). The article originally appeared in *Merkur*, number 213, December, 1965, 1139 bis-1153 according to the note in the Spanish edition we used.

6. Bergson, Henri, "Stating the Problems," in *The Creative Mind*, trans. Mabelle L. Andison (New York: Greenwood Press, 1968), 58-59.

7. Among others Gabriel Marcel, Émile Bréhier, and Miguel de Unamuno have alluded to the distinction between problem and mystery. The two expressions closely correspond to our distinction between question and problem, although we would not identify them in philosophical matters. In this regard, it is important to reproduce an observation by Gabriel Marcel, *Being and Having*, trans. Katherine Far-

rer, intro. James Collins (New York: Harper and Row, 1965); for instance, 100-101, 111, 117. A problem is what we find complete before us, with which we establish an external relation and which we are therefore able to analyze, reduce, or eliminate, whereas mystery (or what *mutatis mutandis* we call questions) involves us personally because it is something that is not entirely before us.

8. Kathleen Freeman, *Ancilla to the Pre-Socratic Philosophers* (Cambridge, Mass.: Harvard University Press, 1948, 1983).

Chapter 3

The Value of Freedom

1. The Constitutive Dimension of Freedom

In all probability freedom is the key concept for approaching an answer to the question of the peculiar being that we are and that we make. No other instrumental notion or group of instrumental notions in the history of thought for grasping anthropological reality seems to wholly reflect the essential structure of human nature and the human mode of existence. The meaning of what we feel, suffer, dream, or hope is not exhausted when we try to characterize it conceptually through our symbolic capability, our rational faculty, our spiritual character, or our diverse empirical (social, political, economic, biological) expressions for our being.

The explanation of what it is to be human certainly ought to contain the characteristics which historically have been offered in definitions. But if we expand the investigation of what makes it possible for humans to involve such modes of being, we must understand that the idea[1] of freedom grounds each one of these conceptual characteristics. If freedom did not specifically constitute the being of man, we would hardly account for any of his least accomplishments, even those which respond to biological impulses or necessities. This is not the place to respond to likely objections. We only urge attentive reflection with truly philosophical spirit (not ideological) on how the qualitative is inherent in every human action and can flower unexpectedly when what is habitual captivates us with sure, impersonal regularity.

The concept of freedom has paradoxically unexpected, constitutive, anthropological wealth. By its denotative depth and universality, it has both greater extension (it embraces the whole species which it signifies) and greater comprehension (it includes the essential notes which express what is specifically human). Diachronically and synchronically, the nuances of freedom involve all possible human experience. Freedom is not simply a characteristic human faculty, but also and above all power of significant unity in which every imaginable human world becomes the concretion—in the Latin sense of *concrescere*—of any imaginable human world.

Acceptance of our approach suggests restoring the concept of freedom to comprehend the meaning of human life and consequently of the totality of human accomplishments. Our project takes its place in the metaphysical order. It is not restricted to the narrow field of the psychological implications of freedom, part of the object of traditional philosophical anthropology. Furthermore, although freedom arises from the ground of human reality, it bypasses the fallacy of examining it in the light of the disjunction "determinism or freedom." Note, however, as fertile matter of further investigations, that our claims are confirmed by the impossibility of calculating reason overtaking it and accounting for it within the limits of its own capacity.

Here, Kant shows us a path, establishing in the third antinomy that natural causality does not contradict freedom, and that, as a postulate of practical reason, freedom is the condition for possibility of moral awareness. Moreover, it is the condition for thinking about the inescapable demands of our natural, human, metaphysical disposition. The dependence of Kant on a restricted concept of reason, however, clouded by modern, scientific triumphalism, made him lose sight[2] of the fact that even in the order of phenomena, of determinism, becoming known was possible by mediation of a prior act of freedom as the foundation of knowledge itself, insofar as the existence of natural, scientific and mathematical knowledge corresponds at bottom to the necessity of coming to know about everything that is. In Kantian terms this means to respond to a natural human metaphysical disposition. If freedom were really only a postulate, an assumption with no deeper guarantee of universality and necessity than the truth of scientific knowledge, we would have a petition of principle.

For the sake of clarity, note that we start with a presupposition, if that is what someone wants to label it, which for us is simply the result of a descriptive examination of what has happened and happens to man in history. The presupposition is that liberty becomes a philosophical problem because it has worth for a particular subject, because this subject supposes that reality has significant importance for him.

By contrast, the efficacy of philosophical analysis is diluted when we want to explain it by appealing to some supraindividual consciousness, Idea, or some similar entelechy. These only suffice to respond to interrogatives about existence intellectually, but hardly serve the goal of showing a firm ground where the metaphysical marginality[3] of human existence nourishes the hope that it will be overcome.

So, concern about the consistency of everything that is becomes possible because this particular man that we are exists, wounded by inevitable finitude. As Max Scheler would have it, he needs to know that he is effectively *at a place* from which he may configure his own image. For that very reason, it follows that any anthropology is logically based in metaphysics, since being human necessarily implies a referential situation toward a *world*. That world is articulated as the other than oneself when significance is accepted in some way, that is, when it acquires a valuation such that it is objectified as presence, and at the same time involves an inevitable response from the flesh and blood subject. The response is decisive, because it may separate him from his personal, human reality or mobilize his ontological potentialities.

2. Actualization of Freedom in Culture

From this perspective, it is clear that freedom is not pure indetermination in the face of natural determination. Nor can all the dimensions of freedom be measured by juxtaposing them partially or wholly to the causal order of phenomena. Nor is it correct to conceive it in extreme terms as absolute and unconditioned.

On the contrary, freedom is configured in successive grades of consciousness as deliberative determination, as historical, situated freedom, of one particular human or a community. Besides, when freedom is mentioned independently of nature, it is because the latter has been emptied of any significant content, it has been reified and neutralized as presence, to the point that it is converted into a strange object ultimately liable to manipulation. A *world* conceived in this way always returns in the form of the depersonalization, deterioration, and destruction of vital human relations, in proportion to the unidimensional consciousness that gave rise to it. This, at least, is the result that can be derived from the experience of will to domination in the history of Western thought.

So, a person posits a world when he signifies nature, for the real in its totality can become present to him only as world. The world thus posited is always cultural order. Nature as radically other, as substantive other configured per se, does not exist *for man* positively. Man can hardly presuppose nature, because in any mode of approximation to nature, it inevitably appears to him as a presence. Nothing can be said of nature in itself which is not already articulated as meaning in the act of saying and is consequently integrated into a culture. Thus, man is necessarily in a cultural world. The totality of the real thus comes to be culture, because, despite being part of nature, the being we are does not live *in* it.

How and why do humans necessarily posit a world? How and why do they make a world appear to them? Doubtless this is what permits a universe of meaning that is capable of situating us, encountering ourselves or knowing ourselves to be meaningfully in a place. It must have a constituent, founding character.

Freedom is precisely the human capacity to signify a world. Given that this world is always a cultural world, it follows that liberty is revealed to us as the very origin of culture. This freedom is the ground from which it is possible to think a response to the meaning of human life, or if one prefers, to its necessarily being placed in a symbolic universe that flowers in meaning and sinks roots in asking.

It follows that culture is the actualization of the specific human capacity, the characteristic and only way in which freedom objectifies itself. This procedure not only permits humans to dispose themselves in a world, signifying their existence, but also opens to them the path to bonding or reconnection with that ground of all grounds by which freedom will achieve the experience of history.

The actualization of a free human nature unfolds in temporality as continuous creation in search of that *plethoric abyss* in which our finitude is reconciled with the infinity of rooted human existence.

Thus, this first movement of transcending freedom posits a world, and the *concern* that the world thus signified should remain as a presence confirms man in the possibility of an ontological leap toward transcendence which is the ground of all grounds.

3. The Veiling of Culture

By way of illustration, northern civilization's metaphysical disintegration, the experience of nothingness and the absurd, is but the experience of how that world emptied of presence is lived. Every possible transcending, every horizon of meaning, is seen as fixed by inescapably immediate finitude, or else it seems to be dissolved in an abyss of ground which despairs of making any sense of it and seeks in anguish to settle itself in the security of *concern* for the "useful," between the promiscuity in ways of behaving and representations of historical mystification.

The alternative for the inhabitant of that industrialized world is to struggle in the exercise of a freedom of doing. This is the path of expanding the realm of the useful, the hegemony of pure externality in the arms race of economic, technological, and political ideological power.

By contrast, cultures historically displaced or restricted by technocratic civilization[4] have a living experience of the radical finitude of existing and even the chaos of a hostile, demoniac world. The living world of such an experience is such an intense present that it always announces the power to be and situates humans in a significant order, in an order of personalized meaning. In these cultures humans enjoyed or still enjoy the possibility of personal communication without misgivings, from existence to existence, because the communities in which man is situated are laden with values that summon his trust. In these communities mere freedom of doing is subordinated to the order of freedom to be, which is, in the communal *we*, transparency of transcending in the direction of ontological plenitude.[5]

4. Community as Development of Freedom

Freedom is man himself. It is also his power. Freedom is primarily power. Abstractly considered, every power in itself is a bundle of possibilities. Possibilities are nothing significant for man without his historical determination, without the effective exercise of this power being carried out temporally in the attempt to realize the dimensions of his existence.

But the power that posits itself in the spatial, temporal order simultaneously entails limitations. If these limitations spring from the actual concern of man for his own transcending, then freedom which is essential to man is ordered to the purpose of his humanization. If the power of freedom does not know how and does not in fact bring out of itself the limitations that human ontological structure necessarily demands, he overflows into the fantasy of an absolute power to do, which is the most serious limitation of freedom, because it turns freedom into its negation under the institutionalized form of tyranny and the spirit of uniformity.

Within a human being there is also the power to elect wretchedness which is a state of soul, failing to accomplish the required possibility of situating its freedom in the order of being by accepting the will to domination as the humanly ultimate in the order of possession. At this point man is entirely submerged by the nature of the useful, and the world signified by it pursues him, in the best of cases,[6] with the irresistible seduction of material gods. Then culture ceases to mediate an encounter with the ground, to be an environment for rootedness and bonding for personal realization. The communication of existences on an ontological level disappears with the triviality and the flash of an instrumental and impersonal contact. The community as an order of persons in free solidarity through the same spirit succumbs as project. In this way man submits to the influence of the abstract universality of a world vision, explicit or not, marked by the expectation of living on the run, without the capacity to elevate one's vision above the weight of contingent circumstances.

Just as community is constituted from the movement of freedom, so also community is the source of freedom, openness, and the ambiance for maturation in the exercise of freedom.

The concepts which serve to define freedom can only be thought independently of the formal examination of reason, because each of them refers to the others in reality and properly is in relation to them. Hence, what follows the development of freedom in the constitution of a community is not the configuration of an order of aggregated parts. False communities are constituted as an aggregation through fear, violence, or some form of despotism; in practice, such societies are born spiritual orphans. An authentic community is a social structure open to transcendence, flourishing from personal assent in which rootedness takes place.[7]

The idea of freedom involves all the possible forms in which that freedom is going to be particularly realized in the process of history. Freedom is simply a constitutive power of the person who posits himself as free in actualization. It is not a self-positing which springs from a pure Self in the manner of a universal, abstract subject, but from an individual originary *we*, primarily undetermined, but which has to develop itself, above all as what it is itself, that is, as it is community. In the effective materialization of community, freedom finds its proportion, because community is neither an obstacle nor compulsion for its growth, but a belonging to an appropriate order, where the direction in which a personal *we* is channeled, traveling in this way the path of bonded participation and empathetic solidarity. Therefore, the destruction of forms of community life, devoured by the crushing uniformity of *the* planetary "civilized" society, will doubtless end by suffocating the development of any personal freedom and with it the encounter of man with himself, if an act of lucidity does not intervene.

Besides, against any reworked nineteenth-century objection that claims community annuls creativity, an authentically communitarian society expands its horizon of meaning simultaneously with human ontological growth at the moment when man finds himself in need and his spirit is swollen with new heavens. Precisely a horizon of meaning is such when it makes apparent the bonding from which man can have at his disposal a significant world for himself.

5. Labor

The factual objectification of freedom is labor insofar as it is the positive sign of the possibilities of the idea of freedom. Human beings retrieve themselves in history using their freedom. This fundamental task in which the purpose of life itself is at stake is accomplished in history. By reason of the human project, history is constituted as the moment of the experience of marginality in which and from which the resurrection of freedom becomes possible if we persevere in the concern for the advent of presence.

But if the exercise of freedom produces work, how then is human work to be understood in this light?

We certainly must not restrict the notion to its socioeconomic factors. Reduction of work to one type of phenomenon, as can occur within the special sphere of economics or sociology, does not reveal the importance of its ontological, existential value for the comprehension of the humans we are.

If we do not investigate beyond its immediate meaning for physical and utilitarian needs, we could be said to cast human concerns into the pit of mere data or appearance without seeing what is posited in that appearance, thus obfuscating the radical human vocation to transcend our biological condition. Not only should work as resolution of freedom in its movement to determination be understood primarily and logically in its full extent as humanly performed activity, but it is nothing less than the mediation of freedom through which culture is constituted historically. There is an essential dialectic between freedom and work, as if they were the obverse and reverse of the same coin.[8] That freedom becomes work temporally and spatially implies the gradual constitution of the world as cultural world in the bosom of a particular community.

Obviously, working denotes occupying oneself with something. This occupying oneself is originally integrally a *disposing* of all of one's being. It is the possibility given to the human being for his encounter with himself (realization of the personal *we*), by transforming and at the same time signifying the real that surrounds him.

As we have explained, in doing this a human being accentuates his personal, creative potency, which is precisely the explicit manifestation of the moment of freedom toward its entire reality. At the same time, work is a *donation*, which, in the desired disposing of oneself, brings solidarity and consistency to a human world. When, however, occupying oneself in something alienates disposition and donation for a simple utilitarian result, in the *some-thing* as goal, then division springs up within man himself. His life is split into an existence for the spirit and another for subsistence, as if there were a possibility of subsisting humanly without the dignity conferred on us to raise ourselves above our finitude![9]

When human effort and activity are not pondered in the light of one's existential, ontological project, but by the measurable value of economic output, the human that we are is alienated in its specific being and creative capacity. We become an instrument of enslavement.

At first sight expressions in many cultures, reinforced by the traditional reading of the Bible, would seem to contradict what we have just said about the idea of labor. But these usages and interpretations— no doubt vitiated by social relations in force at the moment of their formulation—would confirm precisely the contrary: pain, suffering, exhausting, painful effort, tribulation, torture, or else the word is connected to expressions which signify the orphan or slave state. However, in the light of a more attentive and less literal examination, these *historical* meanings allude to the profound and certainly painful experience of finitude, which we have termed "metaphysical marginality."[10]

6. Freedom in History

In the context of our reflection, history is constituted as the environment where *anthropophany* occurs, that is, the appearance and growth of the person as center of ontological irradiation and living presence, by the exercise of freedom.

In this movement of the spirit from corporeality toward infinity, the human reencounters itself as a *we* which completes and totalizes our metaphysically finite existence.[11] The personal *we* which is revealed in attentive, vigilant, devoted living is no longer the primary constitutive *we*, particular and abstract, still empty of determinations which freedom engenders in its developments. The act of freedom has made experience of marginality reside within man and with it the experience of encounter in the search for meaning. The personal *we* comes to make for itself a concrete, fulfilling, whole, open to infinity.

Man journeys from abstract, purely potential freedom to situated freedom (freedom of choice or freedom in the order of doing). From the latter, he can rise to creative freedom of disposition (freedom in the order of being). Mutatis mutandis, he can rise from transiting through homogeneous, de-sacralized space and time to dwell in sacred space and time, whose ontological density assures human life of significance and meaning.

Notes

1. Our approach can be enriched by the Kantian distinction between concept and idea. If the first helps describe what really is when we say "freedom," the other presents itself as a necessity for human activity by its regulative character. In our reflection, freedom as idea also refers to that area of reality which is not exhausted by the limits imposed by pure *ratio ratiocinans*, reasoning reason. It is especially useful to encounter the ground from which everything that is gets consistency. This allows us to approach the beginning of what the human being can hope for, because to ask what it is to be human does not have an adequate answer without this idea. However, any elaboration of an answer, although a specifically philosophical open reflection, will inevitably be conceptual.

Besides, we note that in referring to freedom indiscriminately as concept (from *concipere*) and idea, we want our explanation to conserve its double aspect. As exceeding meaning, it transcends the characteristics of what we habitually call "natural light"; at the same time it is manifested as the unity of meaning from which reason illuminates, comprehends, and covers human accomplishments.

2. That is what the common, academically consecrated, scholastic interpretation suggests. Another reading of Kant might put more emphasis on the order of questions which direct his philosophical project. Our reflection might be the working hypothesis to recuperate a grandly metaphysical Kant, condemned by Kantian scholasticism to be being evaluated on a partial reading of the first Critique. Heidegger must be acknowledged as a philosophical Prometheus on this point, just as Socrates for engagement philosopher in the search for truth. Cf. Martin Heidegger, *Die Frage nach dem Ding* (Tübingen: M. Niemeyer Verlag, 1963), Spanish edition and notes Eduardo García Belsunce and Zoltan Szankay, *La pregunta por la cosa* (Buenos Aires: Editorial Sur, 1964), 230. Heidegger concludes his examination of *The Critique of Pure Reason* affirming: "Kant's asking for the thing asks for intuition and thinking, for experience and its principles, that is to say, asks for man. The interrogative, 'What is a thing?' is the interrogative, 'Who is man?' This does not mean that things are transformed into human fabric, but the reverse. We must comprehend man as he who has always gone beyond things, but in such a way that this going beyond only becomes possible in so far as things go out to his encounter, and thus they remain themselves, in so far as they send us back after ourselves and behind our surface. In Kant's asking for the thing a dimension is opened which lies between the thing and men, which reaches beyond things and behind men."

3. The sociological view of this concept would appear to have no epistemological alternative other than to think of it as mere externality. The limitation of this perspective is to customarily consider marginality as the other of a whole, including the scientist who studies it. However, for us, the marginal always involves the circumstance of being inside a totality, although alien to it. Hence our use of the ex-

pression "metaphysical marginality." Each and every human is marginal in history, because by himself he does not cover the totality of meaning of his existence. He cannot absolutely account for himself. He belongs to the being of the world at the same time as he is alien to it. See H. Daniel Dei, *Bases para una Antropodicea: Acerca del sentido de la vida del hombre* (Buenos Aires: Eros Editor, 1978), 35 ff.

4. "Civilization" is used instead of "culture" because instrumental factors have progressively been exaggerated in such a way that the values which signified the content of culture have been submerged with the consequent loss of rootedness and links in that culture. The logic of every civilizing process is homogenization of differences and symbolic depersonalization of reality.

5. A good example of how a depersonalizing social order lacks the capacity of attracting human trust is the life of Martin Fierro. The protagonist is constantly debased by others who possess a concept of the world that excludes freedom to do and disavows in practice any bonding of a metaphysical character. Despite this persecution, Fierro's concern overcomes the abandonment in which he is cast, because he trusts in a higher order. He appeals to it with a certain shrewd skepticism; the foundational desire for authentic community cries out in him. Among other verses:

> *Su esperanza no la cifren*
> *nunca en corazón alguno;*
> *en el mayor infortunio*
> *pongan su confianza en Dios.*

[Let them never base their hope in some one heart; in the greatest misfortune, let them place their confidence in God.] This illustrates a fundamental aspect of the drama of Argentina and by extension of all Latin America. They are not yet structured by the lived experience of antinomies which partly spring from the attempt to apply a rationality whose underlying pathos cannot be reconciled with the pathos in those on whom that rationality comes to bear.

6. When we exceed in this path of the freedom to do, it can lead man to exaggerate his reflective capacity and annul any trace of resistance by thought. There are tragically abundant past and present historical examples of this unhappy degradation, which threaten to establish themselves planetwide under the appearance and sign of freedom.

7. Our concept of community is not characterized by the relation of identity Hegel sees between the concept of freedom, religion, and state. Hegel says: "In religion human beings are free before God. Because they make their will conform to the divine will, they are not opposed to the highest will, but instead have themselves within it; they are free because in the cultus they have achieved the sublimation of the rupture. The state is simply *freedom in the world*, in actuality. What essentially matters is the concept of freedom that a people bears within its self-consciousness, for the concept of freedom is realized in the state, and the consciousness of freedom, as it is implicitly, belongs essentially to this realization." Georg Wilhelm Friedrich Hegel, *Lectures on the Philosophy of Religion*, vol. 1 (*The Lectures of 1831*), ed. Peter C. Hodgson, trans. R. F. Brown, P. C. Hodgson, and J. M. Stewart, with the assistance of J. P. Fitzer and H. S. Harris (Berkeley: University of California Press, 1984), 452. From our explanation it may be inferred that the identification between state and freedom, or better, the realization of freedom in the state—in the form of something impersonal—is precisely one of the forms in which freedom ends up by being annulled, subsumed in a totalitarian state of whatever kind, but equally depersonalizing. A state constituted in this way would only be the objectified version of a false community according to our definition.

8. Cf. H. Daniel Dei, *Bases para una Antropodicea*, 33.

9. Hence dualistic approaches, matter vs. spirit and its anthropological analogue, body vs. soul, manual labor vs. intellectual work, practice vs. theory, lead nowhere.

10. As a passing illustration of the subsequent development of our position, recall the ancient Latin distinction between *opus* and *labor*. Activity or work is taken as object without pejorative implications, while the various acceptations of *labor* include birth pain and struggling under a great burden.

Here it is useful to ask whether the human task of retrieving ourselves in history, the positive increase of our freedom, is not like the formidable effort of the woman who gives birth to new life, in our context, to meaning. In another order, working can be understood as salvation, as participation in the community to which we belong, sacred insofar as signified cosmos.

11. Our idea is inspired in the relation, which is at the same time one and diverse, between the persons in the Trinity. The correspondence with man is inverse (for obvious ontological, metaphysical reasons) to the absolute relation which is God in the mystery of the Trinity, which might be expressed thus: the Absolute We is revealed as infinity (Father) in historicity (Jesus Christ) as communication which is comprehensible to us through love (Holy Spirit).

Chapter 4

Anthropodicy: The Question of Man

1. Search for Truth versus Legitimation of Truth

The search for truth is only a *search*. This statement is far from obvious; it involves a position on fundamental themes which have divided men throughout history. We will not attempt an academic presentation here. We simply hope to clarify our argument. By affirming that search for truth is only a search, we situate ourselves *before* any answer about *what is* truth. This is the first and most important proposition in our invitation to open an area of reflection about the meaning of life.

Indeed, the only thing evident is that *some* truth exists, even if we imagine it in the form of a negative proposition. We do not aspire to legitimate any answer about truth. Legitimation is an unavoidable personal task for each human. The history of mankind is nothing but the realization of certain truths that we interpret as such and that we have sometimes justified by reason, other times by force, and almost always by feeling, though most of the time we have lacked the *disposition* for the search.

Even if the difference in attitude is clear between *legitimating a truth*, that is, appealing to some mode of grounding that truth on the base of knowledge, and *searching for the truth*, insofar as setting out in the confidence that an answer may become apparent at some point, it is still not obvious what we refer to as truth here. Do the two activities share any presupposition besides the use of the word "truth"? Surely, they share what is thought when we use the term. The difference in attitudes is largely justified by the sense "truth" has here, which is its most problematic sense of *meaning*.

But what other acceptation could be involved in treating the question of man? What else is sought or is legitimated amid all human grandeur or misery but to configure a meaning for individual or collective actions?

Culture is produced by this configuration of meaning, ordering the chaotic, discovering or imposing legality and permanence in what is manifested as contingent and a matter of chance. *All* religious expressions and *all* efforts of science and philosophy acknowledge this agonistic human project. If we look more closely, we discover it is the way each of us lives his daily life either when we accept an order of meaning in which we are involved or when we attempt to re-signify our situation within that order. Even at the extremes of the rupture of all ordering, in mystical flight, philosophical nihilism, suicide, or mental illness, there is truth, present as the meaning of the world. We certainly could not live without some meaning, without an elementary ordering of the chaotic.

2. Reiteration of a Necessary Clarification of Language

We have presupposed the universal character of the human search for truth. But is our discourse mere conjecture tied to our philosophical perspective or does it bring out a need derived from man's very ontological condition?

The history of ideas offers answers that range from accepting natural necessity in the search for truth to affirming that the search is mere fiction, a dream to compensate for our helplessness. In reality these extremes are not contradictory. Beyond legitimating pretensions, they reflect an answer about the meaning of life. It does not help the diversity of opinions to add one more. To situate the question of man thematically it does seem useful to determine the point where differences begin and from there to re-create the possibility of a zone of encounter. We must first investigate what ontological condition we share by virtue of being men that we cannot evade even though we try. This examination will better prepare us to confront the decisive act of undertaking the inescapable *personal* reply to these interrogatives.

Everyone already has a position on these topics, reflectively or irreflectively. We could not live without a certain meaningful appropriation or configuration of the reality in which we are placed. Still, we feel it is necessary to repeat a distinction about types of solutions we can expect.[1]

A sure source of philosophical and human prephilosophical disagreement, which affects the production of knowledge about human accomplishments, is the failure to distinguish between a *problem* and what is properly a *question*.

"Question" is an interrogative which in the very act of being formulated opens perspectives of meanings in the interrogator. By contrast, we face a problem when there is an unknown which is simply removed by a datum that we lack, but which may plausibly appear in time.

Questions and problems illustrate paths toward the comprehension of the world. They orient in investigation and the search for truth. But the doubts that move the interrogatives we call questions are never exhausted by a definitive answer, nor do they resolve themselves positively in the manner of answers in the sciences or about everyday concerns. What science and even ordinary knowledge make clear with their replies depends on the opportunity for information and the quality of instruments available in a stage of development or a specific circumstance.

It is worth noting that this last affirmation does not suggest that every question can be resolved by science or will be at some point of future time, because science is not concerned with questions—in our sense—but with problems. When the scientist in his thirst for knowledge goes deeper and transcends the limits of the presuppositions upon which his particular discipline rests, he is obliged to formulate philosophical considerations of a metaphysical order, with the handicap of sometimes lacking the necessary preparation or of employing the same approach and analogous techniques in his analysis as he did in scientific problems. We see this in the ultimate interrogatives—questions—which scientific investigations pose in astrophysics, cosmology, physics, biochemistry, or genetic biology, as well as neurophysiology, paleontology, or zoology.

If problems are basically obstacles discovered in our contact with reality they are obviously solved when we dispose of the necessary information or knowledge in the framework of an adequate, specific methodology. By contrast, questions, interrogatives about meaning, accompany us like our own body. They involve us existentially, and they demand a *re-solution*, a personal decision of our freedom.

What answer, then, can satisfy traditional philosophical questions about being, the world, and man? For example when we ask, "What is life?" from our experience of life itself, we do not expect an explanation of biological phenomena. What is at stake behind this sort of interrogative is the ultimate meaning of our presence in the world and the sense of our accomplishments. In other words, we are looking for an individual, personal answer which contains what is truly implicit in the interrogation. The interest in what can happen with my life is not primarily abstract, intellectual, or speculative. Once I have an answer for myself, the necessity of its universalization, that is. to legitimate it, will appear.

This explains the diversity of opinions that we find in philosophy; also, how unjust it is to declare that philosophy is useless when, from authenticity, it abstains from positive, closed answers. Strictly, for those who try to cultivate philosophy, the great philosophical questions are always the same. What appears as a sign of contradiction is exactly the human capacity to give answers as rich as they are diverse, at the same time as to formulate them situationally, in a determined space and time, which is to say, according to an ontological horizon of the man who accepts them in thinking.

Consequently, if problems concern science, philosophy, by contrast, occupies itself with questions, with interrogatives about meaning. To involve us in interrogatives which stem from posing the question of man is to call us to meditate the deep existential cares that come from the very fact of being human. In some measure, that is, to dispose us to travel the path of philosophy.

3. The Tasks of Philosophical Anthropology and the Sciences of Man

With more prudence than precision, people speak about the "sciences of man" referring to the investigation of physical and sociocultural issues centering on man as object of their problematic. However, these disciplines at their core, sometimes lumped together as "social sciences" or "human sciences," refrain from unilateral positions in the problematic of man, without totally relinquishing their specific methodological contributions.

Nowadays generalization from a partial empirical and theoretical base is not admissible even in physical sciences. One of the most important contributions of the natural sciences in the twentieth century has been to accept a cosmological perspective in which consideration of the totality of phenomena is decisive; the singular, individual fact only becomes intelligible when it is inserted in that totality.

With greater reason, when we attempt to discuss man, an integrating vision is not only more and more indispensable but it turns out to be consistent with the internal dynamics and foreseeable evolution of the disciplines which make up the corpus of the social sciences. Therefore, an integrating approach toward man, which saves his singularity without losing sight of the symbolic and material context in which that singularity is manifested, must rid itself of the empty universalization characteristic of scientism or any rationalist schematic and simultaneously attempt philosophically to situate the question of man.[2]

So, the task of anthropology is inseparable from this interdisciplinary effort, because it can not only supply the radical interrogatives which discover theoretical presuppositions in particular sciences, but also show the ontological, existential position of the being we call man. To situate the question of man is, in principle, to situate the interrogative metaphysically, to deal with the *what* and *why* of his existence. Everything else is description, approximation, trial balloons, which permit us to understand, even to "explain" his manner of being and acting in the world.

4. Philosophical Investigation and Man's Daily Concerns: Life as Human Possibility

Like any knowledge that we men can develop, philosophy never lacks presuppositions. Academic tradition has accustomed us to the notion that it is presuppositionless knowledge. However, it is helpful to rapidly note that this is not a rigorous expression when it expresses more than pedagogical intentions. Indeed, its validity is debatable even for purposes of helping those who wish to know how philosophy's principles differentiate it from science. The claim is less precise and clear than the prevailing distinction made by Plato in the *Republic*.

The only presupposition of knowledge which aspires to be nonhypothetical is the living project of being disposed to whatever may appear on our path, of flowing into new interrogatives which open new horizons of meaning. To think radically and systematically is certainly to philosophize, but only if it is an experience of intensely and consciously living the possibilities of every instant, in which the certainties of today are the uncertainties of tomorrow and onward, at the same time as we build up a storehouse which maintains our history, the memory of an ever-present identity. Consequently, every general philosophical investigation takes up the daily concern of man to be more than a *given*—a chance variable with only the dignity of his niche in the evolutionary cycle.

But philosophism, just like scientism, is a pathology of omnipotent reason. Transformed into ideologies, they are apt to spring up in the search for truth. They constitute a state of hubris, the sin of intellectual pride which pushes us to go beyond the modest condition of our knowledge and erase differences. They are confined spaces which our fears construct to avoid the slippage of the line of the horizon. With them perseverance fades from a spirit which had been disposed for the mystery of life. In the end, the door is opened to lose the roots which ground our daily toils. In science as in life, that is the scattering of lucidity.

Here we are trying to affirm the value of life. For life to be a value in itself, we must respect the mystery of its possibility. Life, and not something else, is our possibility. To make it a human opportunity is our only meaningful task, if we make the decision that it should reveal its secrets to us.

5. Meaning of the Question: What Is Man?

We are facing a question about essence, in this case the essence of man. What is this business about the "essence" of man? Does the interrogative presuppose a truth about which it asks? Clearly, if we ever imagined that the interrogative was closed, purely rhetorical, the present study would not have been written. We are not interested in talking about man's essence. This is already a matter of controversy in the history of philosophical schools.

According to our methodology, the claim that man has or lacks an essence would imply in fact the assumption of an answer to the question which drives our reflection. Should we, then, reformulate what we have asked? Not at all. Our commitment to what we ask is the asking. It puts us on the path to investigate what happens in the interrogation. If we are in the presence of a question, we must be consequent with the disposition of allowing ourselves to be carried along by what appears there without precipitation, without previous judgments or hypotheses about the result.

How should we value what we have asked? That is, how should we speak of its meaning, without committing ourselves to some philosophical position?

Let us revisit what is implied in a question. The fundamental thing about an interrogative of this sort is the character of what we ask. When we ask, "What is man?" we find ourselves involved in all of the dimensions of possibility of our existence. Although we ask formally in universal terms, the immediate resonance confounds the intelligence and demands that we situate our thought in the total universe of our individual life. Any suggestion of a merely intellectual reply is felt to be empty, abstract, incomplete. The asking submerges us in the naked, lived experience of our existence as it happens, the lived experience of this being that we are. The environment defined by our social personality becomes blurry, and a silence of concepts, labels, categories, and truths is opened. We involve ourselves in a silence of formidable ontological repercussions. Not chaos but the abyss or the totality—as one prefers—of the manifestation of the being of existence with all its interrogatives becomes present to us. And without any simulation, this is the most significant response: knowing we are an interrogative, asking for meaning.

6. An Inescapable Personal Reply and the Contribution of Philosophy

Although the lived experience of asking submerges us in uneasy uncertainty, it opens a horizon of new concerns about all the truths that sustain us in daily life. Above all, it leaves us with the experience of a different, substantive connection with reality, an ontological connection. What matters is not whether this reality is the product of our imagination. It is important to stress that the experience of living the interrogative about what we are refers to the "reality" of being in what we call "world" and that, whether or not it is an illusion, the issue is decisive even for the most trivial things in which we place our confidence.

Before continuing, we want to deal with an objection from "practical realism." Far from being the same prudent common sense in these matters, practical realism usually does the evil service of discounting the interrogative's practical transcendence—*practical*, we repeat—relegating it to the zone of leisure or theoretical pastimes. Our asking and answering are always active, in the more elementary or transcendent decision to continue living. But repeatedly asking lets us become aware that we are living and—if we have an answer—lets us remake the decision for the broad horizoned answer about why we live and for what we live. The moment of explicit interrogative is an unpredictable circumstance as is its formal expression. Those who are most intellectual worry about the syntactic appropriateness, the elimination of vague, ambiguous terms, semantic details, or linguistic precision, and so forth, but the shock to us of the presence of the question is like the inevitability of death. The same feeling of existential anguish, astonishment, and communication with the mystery of life, with the mystery of everything that is, banishes if only for an instant, our elaborate psychological constructions. If we draw a lesson from opportune ontological lived experience, the valuation of our actions and our anxieties for things will doubtless be different.

This practice of living is grounded in the inescapable, personal, continual response of assenting to life. The assent's personal character is even expressed when we evade an entirely conscious and reflective response about life. The negation of life has only one authentic, logically valid consequence which is suicide. Its verbalization is mere narcissism or pathology, though innumerable examples of this pathology are to be found in the political history of humanity with a corresponding legitimation in the history of philosophical ideas.

The question about what we are is equivalent to the question about the meaning of life, since we are dealing with *our* life, no more and no less. Our asking points to a response about the meaning that we want to *read* regarding what we are. This business is nontransferable. The contribution of philosophy is to prepare us to travel the road.

7. Our Proposal: Anthropodicy

"Anthropodicy is the name we gave to our philosophical perspective in 1978.[3] The word consists of the Greek ανψροποω (anthropos), human being or man in general, and δικ↓ (*dike*) justice. Our object is the justification of anthropos, to defend him δ⇔κην ειπε⇑ν (*díken eipeîn*). The point of the neologism is not to differentiate our position from others. The expression indicates a clear, rigorous program that attempts philosophical reflection about man starting from its ultimate possibility; having opened the interrogative for meaning, the point is to let oneself be carried by the interrogating itself, to examine what we can share independently of our resolutions to the point of discovering when and why the streams separate and hermeneutic divergence appears.

Only the experience of a sincere disposition on the path *dis-poses* us, that is, makes *two facta appear* to us. Two facts make it possible to confront the flesh-and-blood man we are in asking what we are. These facts are: (1) our ontological, existential condition and (2) the necessity of making the symbolic universe in which we live significant. If our project has merit it is precisely the absence of a positive reply to the question of man—at least one deliberately pre-elaborated. For we understand that our task, and the task of philosophy, is essentially propaedeutic. We have imposed this prudent limitation on ourselves, since our conversation will stop when we notice that the exercise of our own personal response is unavoidable.

From a different perspective that we will not develop here, anthropodicy as a reflective, systematic approach criticizes positive modes of thinking the question of man and the sense of reality itself, which a specific, different line of work in philosophy or the history of ideas has bequeathed to us. By contrast when anthropodicy poses the question of man as the proper theme of philosophy, without disguising its methodological difficulties, it permits transparent witness to a practice of philosophizing consubstantial with the ultimate concerns of man. Initially it does not wish to remove its gaze from the moving, revealing experience of our metaphysical condition by parting from the great topical subterfuges like God, Being, History, Will to Power, etc. If there is something we must *justify* in the world it is our presence. *All* history of mankind is just an intrepid effort to legitimate the destiny of this presence.

We can have a better understanding of this approach if we pose the question with the following scheme:

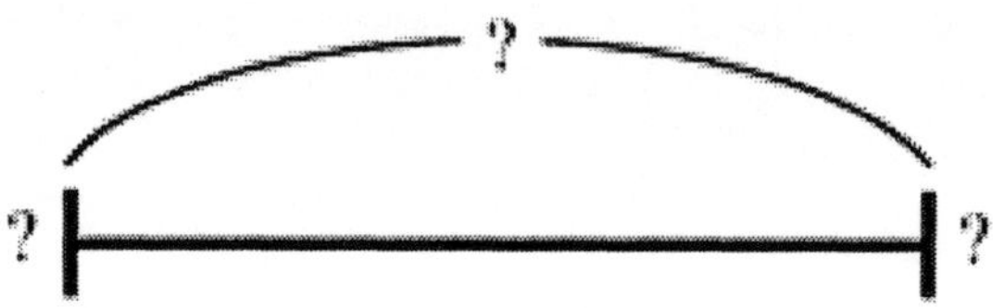

The segment represents our history, our lives placed between two question marks. The only certainties which seem to escape an act of faith about the sense are that we exist in this temporal space represented by the segments at whose extremes are birth and death, origin and end. But the whole segment is also a great interrogative. When we elaborate a response to the sense of this history, we also respond to the question of the origin and the end. In other words, we can share the observation that just as we have been born at a time and place, in another time and place that we ignore we are *necessarily* going to die.

Without doubt we complete a cycle which goes between something that we were not, at least not as we are, and something that we surely will not be in the same manner as we have been. We call that cycle our life. What we do not know is about the destiny, the meaning, or the direction of our presence in this circumstance. Therefore, this human life reclaims its finality, even when we come to admit that the alternative might be the vanity of the pretension. This is so evident that it admits no objection, because the presence of the interrogative and its response taint every one of our actions. Hence the path of anthropodicy, that is, the process of justification of what in truth we are, constitutes the necessary point of reference for humans in every legitimating discursive appeal, whether practical or theoretical.

8. The Path of Asking about the Meaning of Our Existence: A Phenomenology of Our Ontological Experience

The facts we have mentioned are revealed to us in the naked lived experience of the question about what we are. Indeed, our ontological, existential condition, and the exposition of an inevitable, virtual, exercise of meaning of that condition, stand as first answer—the first and decisive answer, because everything that we subsequently say about ourselves and about what constitutes our circumstances will depend on the direction that the answer takes. But this condition which is revealed in the question does not ground what exists (in reality we cannot know if it does), but rather it presents to us the problematic dimension of our existence and the constitutive position from which it is possible to think something. The interpretation of the phenomenon, that is, what is going to give meaning to our existence, arrives because of an originary act of signification. In the lived experience of interrogation, only the reality of what we are is opened to us, independently of the determinations which configure our specific psycho-genetic or historical situation—contents of a "preconscious argument or plan of life" which is psychological in nature. That is why the experience is entirely ontological.

What is this originary reality that manifests itself to us as such, without factual thematization or legitimation? First of all, that we are subject to the permanent paradox of change. The characteristic of our mode of being is contingency. Everything that affects us would seem to vanish in the abyss of the contingent. As we explained, at one time our existence was not, at least as it is now, and what we are and are not when we speak will cease to be at our death. However, our gaze cannot sustain itself in the contemplation of what is not. Nothingness as possibility of phenomenological description immediately is seen as deceitful, not only because we are, even if no more than some contingency *trying* to be, but because "we feel" that the interrogation has also asked about the permanent which is hidden in the anguish of the lived experience of contingency. Moreover, the same interrogation about what we are reveals that it is constructed by the concern for a noncontingent "presence." We cannot imagine asking in all intensity without the concern for permanence. Even if we may rationally deny the value of the asking, the asking is there before us always.

From the perspective of anthropodicy, one of the modes in which our ontological, existential condition shows itself is the lived experience of the contingent character of our existence. The determination of that contingency, that *we pass* from non-being to being and from being to non-being, as "nothingness," is already the product of the intervention of freedom which has made the *fact* significant. The lived experience has been understood by the mediation of freedom which has imposed *a* sense upon our condition. But this is a possible sense that we can give. Indeed man has given himself other senses. The personal task to which we invite is precisely to configure this lived experience meaningfully.

It still remains to find what is discovered as "non-contingent presence" or "concern for permanence" and what links make it appear with the lived experiences of our proceeding from non-being to being. Anthropodicy proposes the phenomenology of ontological experience to clarify how and when the *interpretative* task begins (the exercise of freedom) in every existence and upon what common experience of our ontological position this task is accomplished.

9. Finitude and Infinitude

Our existence is unavoidably subject to this lived experience of contingency. Phenomenologically considered, the experience is simply the proper manifestation of our finitude in a world also revealed as finite. By stressing the experience of contingency as finitude we advance conceptually toward the very phenomenon which has overtaken us in the path of interrogation.

Now we know ourselves situated in a horizon which unfolds in possibilities that open at birth and close at death, in a space and time we do not choose, in a life which nevertheless demands our assent to be lived. We have appropriated the lived experience and have categorized it as finitude. Thereby, the *fact* has become intelligible to reason: it is a *datum* of our existential reality, of our peculiar condition as beings in the world. But this datum is still originary, because it is sustained in the continuity of what is essentially manifested in the *fact*. The datum does not alter the fact; it does not interpret it; it only permits that it be exposed to thought.

Furthermore, the apprehension of our being as finitude does not uniquely make the peculiarity with which our ontological condition becomes present to consciousness. Rather, this is done by the ambivalence of the mode of being of our existence. Together with contingency, that mode shows the necessity of being in the identity of an ontological permanence, of sustaining itself beyond incessant change, and of understanding itself in the direction of a destiny. We call "aspiration to infinity" that presence of a noncontingent *something* which struggles to thread an articulation in the successive, continual movement from *being thus* to *being in another way*. "Aspiration to infinity" makes thinkable and communicable that human need of going beyond the *fact* of contingency. It is worth noting that the term "infinity" does not necessarily indicate an extra-worldly reality nor the realization of an absolute in the immanence of the order of things. For the moment it simply says transcendence, the desire to overcome the finite condition of existence, the vocation of plenitude, and to shake off the inconsistency of our ontological constitution.

Even in a deepened perspective on the experience of finitude, the very nature of the movement of contingency manifests being as the possibility of something presented as fluctuating and contradictory. In other words, the finite can only be comprehended if we refer to what there is of being in its movement. This finite-infinite dialectic expresses the ambivalence of our existence. Life, our life, is a permanent tension in search of sense. It flows pregnant with death, uneasy amid fears and limitations, without more consistency than passing and watching for the encounter with a meaningful horizon.

10. An Ontological Definition of Man

Hence, when it is asked what man is, it is untenable to respond by giving a definition which would close the interrogative to new investigations. The asking has the character of a question. A question requires an approximation to go beyond the natural, phenomenal, classical determination of the being that we are, which still does not exude that determination as possible. Thus, we propose to approach a new *ontological* definition of man, which would really attempt to conceptualize what the experience of interrogation unveils in our ontological, existential condition.

Definitions of man which start with animality are doubtless necessary, if we accept a limited range of application, but they do not get behind considering man as a natural being, even when we broaden the comprehension of the concept with diverse specific differences (rational, metaphysical, symbolic, social, political, religious, and so forth) proposed in the history of philosophy, all complementary in the last analysis. These definitions do not take up the lived human *facts* in his ontological experience that gives rise to the interrogative. Consequently, the question of the sense of man's existence is hidden. Man has before him a legitimating curtain upon which he can shift the responsibility of making his assent to life lucid. Nevertheless, the interrogative dwells with us, it is always open to what befalls us unexpectedly in the virtual continuity of existence. Then the question returns once and again in the guise of a discussion which is inescapable and belongs to each one.

As we have seen, to ask about what man is, cannot be likened to asking about just any being. It is above all an investigation in which a *who* is involved situated in the finite-infinite tension. That is, a someone conscious of the radical finitude of his being not yet achieved in its possibilities but which aspires to be constituted in the full unity of its existence. The nature of our asking demands something more than to specify an essence so as to set apart man in the world as a being among other beings. It summons us to an ontological approximation which opens a horizon of sense to one who is involved in the search without renouncing the inevitable answer that he must give. What permits man to become thinkable in a concrete universal, in a concept nourished by the experience of what happens to him when he travels the path of interrogation, is the particularity of his metaphysical condition as finite being. Therefore, unlike other beings we might imagine, man is a finite being with aspirations to infinity. The *eros* which moves man to cross his own limits will find a destiny in the exercise of freedom.

11. What We Know and Do Not Know about Ourselves: Situation and Dense

We know we are finite, limited, situated in a determined space and time. Our finitude consists precisely in the inconsistency of our being (or in whatever we discover about ourselves when we ask). We are subject to change, but not in the manner of a mobile which goes from one end of a line segment to the other. We are an otherness which contains identity as the condition of its most intimate possibility of change. That otherness is strange. That identity is even stranger, for it imposes contingent absolutes and permanent presences which are ruptures of any illusion of permanence: there is continuity of becoming of our existence and there is temporality with its burden of irreversible death and of what arrives irremissibly. The simple idea of life includes death among its possible manifestations. These possibilities are not elective in the manner of a freedom of option. It is not that they *can* be accepted. They *must* be accepted and objectified as the *praxis* of life in some direction thanks to the exercise of another kind of freedom. *Eros* is situated as aspiration of completion, plenitude of being, life or meaning of existence; it bares the tension of the ambivalence of our metaphysical constitution rising up from our ontological poverty as the impulse of transcendence.

This is what we know about ourselves. This is what phenomenological examination reveals as constitutive of our existence, as the metaphysical condition of our being. What is it, then, that we do not know about ourselves? What is it that engenders such diverse points of view about what we are?

Anthropodicy lets us recognize that man is a finite being, that he shares the metaphysical structure of the other beings of the universe in which he is placed. Unlike them, he aspires to infinitude. The consciousness of the need to surpass his own limits giving meaning to his condition is inherent in his finite condition. This is the mystery of man. It is the glory and tragedy of his ontological destiny. He cannot be without a meaning, without some truth that sustains him metaphysically. Life for man is always life in a world, living existence in a determined order of meaning. What we do not know about ourselves is precisely what this truth or this meaning is. It is the great unknown which is uncovered in the lived experience of interrogation. We find this need to respond is fact, this need to resolve what we have asked in the horizon of comprehension opened by interrogation about what we are. The answer to these new interrogations is the inescapable, untransferable task which each person must accomplish in his life and thereby find his destiny. Within the possibilities of our freedom is the direction which the interpretation of the world and life takes, and with this interpretation the historical fleshing out of our existence.

12. Response to What We Do Not Know: The Exercise of Freedom

What we do not know is the meaning of life, the *truth* of our presence in the world. We do know that biologically there are two unavoidable instants, birth and death. Furthermore, we infer that there is phylogenetic continuity and ontogenetic development. Nowadays, we have a more coherent description of the universe, and the perfection of methods and the instrument of observation will permit us to improve that description. Historical memory links our existences to other, similar existences in time. However, that biological and historical memory and the awareness of the astounding expansion of the frontiers of science is insufficient. We urgently need to *know ourselves* to be historical, to leap over explicative hypotheses and *situate ourselves* meaningfully above the *fact* of our finite condition. Questions are present independently of progress in our knowledge. Paradoxically, the more we know about processes and things, the greater our unease and urgency to get an answer about the meaning of events.

Life is no less an enigma now than in the remote ages of our presumed ancestors. Perhaps some fears of our primitive and not so primitive brethren no longer perturb us, but we certainly face tragic metaphysical uncertainty. Awareness of this tragedy has grown in every direction: from the modest aspiration to transcendence by continuing the species despite the real threat of planetary destruction, to the idea of fullness of life after death despite generalized adulteration of the sacred and the facility of the manipulation of value in the present life. Individual existence and the world of human existence are, therefore, one unique interrogative about meaning which seems to wander toward the uncertain in a horizon without roots, one of fictitious and provisional possibilities.

For what are we chained here and now between inevitable origin and end, in absolute contradiction of our necessity to be in plenitude? Whither hasten all our solicitudes? What logic obliges us to wager on that obstinacy about permanence when awareness of finitude shakes the departments of our psychological securities and permeates the most minute projects with uncertainty?

Despite everything, we have discovered an indisputable point of departure. We know we are finite beings, but unlike any other being, our finitude is constituted in the positing of *human life*; that is to say, in the necessity of assenting to its character of a project not determined by its nature.

The path of anthropodicy is the path of fidelity to what presents itself to us in the interrogation for what we are; it permits us to be aware of the landscape implicit in what we take as obvious. It reveals that we know nothing beyond the segment of existence which is our life between birth and biological death which is not already a postulation of meaning, an effect of the exercise of our fundamental, ontological freedom. So, we are on the threshold of interpretative differences about the truth of everything that is; at the point of inflection that gives way to legitimations which sustain our aspirations in life and in which we ground hopes of full achievement of our existences. This necessary postulation of meaning is revealed to be demanded by our very ontological condition in the lived experience of asking what we are. The answer to what we do not know depends on the actualization of this freedom, whose essence is understood as the capacity of meaning. Through it we configure a world, an order, a symbolic universe which makes that contingent segment of unavoidable existence that we are a project of life.

13. Metaphysical Marginality and Historicity of Our Existence

This response to what we do not know is the response of meaning. Our existence aspires to that response in order to grasp itself in human life's historical project. When life is affirmed, logically, it is always affirmed as human life.

Therefore, by nature this freedom is the ground. In its constitutive act of positing itself as liberty, it entails a complete axiology of the world we want. It might be maintained that the determination of willing as free choice or psychological freedom depending on free choice serves for human acting, but that is not required in the interrogation experience. The affirmation of life is the assent of our freedom to the possibility of achieving ourselves in the fullness of being, of responding to the aspiration of infinitude. This aspiration not only situates us in the permanence demanded when we ask what we are; without it we literally could not live; it moves our existence to transcend its own limits. The other existences are implicated in the exercise of our ontological freedom. *We are* in an originary community of belonging and destiny, humanity, which also makes itself present to us in its most radical condition of being in the ambiguity of the finite-infinite tension. Accordingly, *we are not* existence submitted to chance in anguished loneliness, but historical, a *we* which must be acknowledged in a world whose project character cannot be doubted. So to speak, we bet our lives in it, the meaningful burden of all our solicitudes.

Humanity is not revealed in our analysis as an abstract universal, a generic entity. To be a community of existences, to be *human*, is the destiny that we accept through liberty to render an account of ontological rootlessness, of the lack of consistency of our most intimate being. This destiny—we repeat—is achieved in a concrete history, in a temporal segment which goes from one point to the other of our life.

Precisely in history we articulate the fact of that contingency of our being which must be denied as pure becoming, as the abstract totality of possibilities, in order to be in the totality of meaning of a world where we live together and that is livable together. But this history is not the *other* of the inescapable necessity of overcoming rootlessness. The history itself is rent by finitude which inheres in our existences. Indeed, man and history are in marginality. We know ourselves by belonging to a universe of meaning, but at the same time, we are incapable of perfectly accounting for it. This is the metaphysically marginal condition of our existences and of history itself, as the *topos* of *anthropophany*, a setting for the manifestation of the human in all its drama, the reason for the unfolding of our aspiration to infinity in the plenitude of a meaningful existence.

14. History as Anthropodicy

As we discovered, the response to that summons to meaningful totality revealed to us when we ask what we are is a *leap* of the *freedom of being* over the *fact* of unappealable finitude of existence. This human manifestation of our specific condition occurs both in individual and collective history. Both have as their fundamental purpose to justify, *díken eipeîn*, to pronounce—and achieve—the defense of our presence in the world before ourselves. The defense is legitimation, which means giving consistency to all our actions, endow the possibilities of our existence with a body of meaning, in the movement of creative transcendence which is at stake in our ontological freedom. Unlike any other way of thinking, anthropodicy situates the question of man as the central theme of investigation. Its methodological point of departure is the key to sorting out what a classical philosophical distinction calls "truths of fact" and "truths of reason." The only truth of fact for which we can *effectively* account is the finite character of our existence. This is what we have attempted here. The other truths that we configure starting with the consciousness of that finitude are reasons which we must necessarily and legitimately postulate in order to live.

15. A Task That Cannot Be Renounced: Differences Which Separate Men

The first stage of the road we have traveled has permitted us to clarify what constitutes the point of inflection where our differences about the meaning of life are born. These differences function in *res gestae*, history as succession of events, as unceasing construction of spaces of power, spaces of identity, which reinforce our aspirations to infinity and suppress the contingent character of our ontological position in culture. We live for the truths that sustain us, and we are also capable of dying for them. Death completes the meaning of existence, if it is sustained by a life wager. But, although we share the same metaphysical uncertainty, and we are tossed about in the inevitable achievement of a human destiny, the task of interpreting the sign of our ontological, existential condition is personal and unique in every case.

Our hope from birth to the plenitude of existence depends on the wager of our freedom of being. To signify the natural life which we are as human life is a necessary task that cannot be delegated. However, only from the acceptation of a world as one's own, from the roots of a horizon of personal meaning, can we open ourselves to the hope of other men to be and exist in plenitude.

16. Prelude to Communication

If the exercise of freedom is the act that constitutes a world which makes the experience of existing valuable and possible, and if the awareness of ontological marginality of our being finds us involved in a common destiny, the differences which separate us could be interpreted as the warp of infinite possibilities of being which are given to us. The majority of men drown that warp out of fear in the face of death. For these fears drown the mystery of life in us and so confuse the dimension of the only real thing for which we can effectively account, that the condition of the existence we are is drama, with fleeting enthusiasm for the construction of psychological absolutes. We suffer the tribulation of the times, and we live absent from joy in its possibilities. Far from suffocating our fears, we feed them slithering along in the dregs of apparent freedom that we win at the cost of others.

However, the path of anthropodicy, of the search for the response to the question of meaning, insinuates to us that this tension between nothing and everything, the contingent and the permanent, the finite and infinite which inhabits our possibilities of being, is fecundated by the exercise of ontological liberty capable of raising up a world above chaos. Disposing ourselves for the discovery of a wealth of meanings of life in the plurality of possible words that each one of us signifies from the cultural circumstance in which we are situated will permit us to re-create a horizon of encounters in a near future. That horizon would be emancipated from sandcastles of universalist legitimations which still separate us as victims and victimizers. For this exchange of world is an exchange of cultural universes that carve out a place between Heaven and Earth with similar longing. If this is so, then the reflection to which anthropodicy summons us has been useful as a prelude to communication, in as far as all human communication is only achievable in an encounter of existences.

Notes

1. The distinction was explicitly made in chapter 2, "The Sense of Philosophical Investigation," section 5. See also chapter 5, "Power and Freedom in Postmodern Society," section 2, in the present work.

2. Our essay, *La Objetividad en Ciencias Sociales* (Buenos Aires: Marymar Ediciones, , 1987), may be consulted for an explanation of how an anthropological perspective serves as an epistemological approach to the social realm and the development of social sciences.

3. H. Daniel Dei, *Bases para una Antropodicea: Acerca del sentido de la vida del hombre* (Buenos Aires: Eros Editor, 1978). A complementary and enriching use of the same expression developed independently of our 1978 effort, is found in Ricardo Maliandi, "La crisis de nuestro tiempo y la dialéctica de la desconfianza," *Escritos de Filosofia* (*Journal of the Center of Philosophical Studies of the Academy of Sciences of Buenos Aires*), no. 12, July-December 1983, 88-89. Maliandi attempts to search for those values which justify the persistence of mankind and shows how philosophical anthropology turns into "anthropodicy."

Chapter 5

Power and Freedom in Postmodern Society: Preliminary Remarks

The social imperative of our time seems to insist that we can all imagine what ought to be learned and what is useful for life. Yet, few people imagine that before beginning to learn it is necessary to assume the *disposition* to do so. Our usual notion of freedom and of power seems to assure us that there is no need to embark on a journey of discovery and wonder in order to reach what we already know. Indeed, consumerism reaches not only material goods but also cultural activity in general and theoretical knowledge in particular. In this context, philosophical reflection comes in as an auxiliary to the great paradigms competing in the marketplace of ideas and becomes unpleasantly "metaphysical," that is, expendable, when it tries to ask freely and rigorously about the sense of the reality we are constructing. Such, nevertheless, will be our intention in the present work. Like any genuine, transparent reflection, ours will be a reflection situated in the backdrop of our lived experience, Argentina, and more generally Latin America at the start of the third millennium.

Law enters philosophical discussion as *pre*occupation for the future. As it should be, this is a fundamental concern of philosophy of law. In the discussion of legal and moral knowledge, we attempt to stress the issue of whether we as philosophers of law are capable of blazing trails for the reflection about future society, instead of discoursing retrospectively about what the study of law and the development of society have "settled" already. However, against what might appear initially, we do not intend to polemicize. If we may say so, everything polemical will rather be an impassioned summons to a shared meditation on a level which lets imagination sketch new horizons and elevate itself to a look

51

forward. We would only request, as Sallust[1] makes Cato say, *animus in consulendo liber*, a free spirit in deliberating. Here interrogatives are more important than declarations. What matters is the place from which varied desirable answers motivate new perspectives for knowledge and better possibilities of imagining our coming humanity rather than preparing a place for customary misencounters of competing schools of thought. We need alternative anthropological models for the deepest human aspirations; since the challenge of the future no longer lies on a comfortable, foreseeable route.

1. History and Future

History is less memory of the past than the circumstance from which the possibility of the future arises. In other words, history is the ground where the future we shape can take root. When this future arrives without our fingerprints, we cease to make our history, but become marginalized from it. In this case the development of specifically human potentialities evaporates into the impersonality of a meaningless life. Man is history, achieved temporality, as long as he confronts what is most characteristic of his nature. Mutatis mutandis, this can be applied to the lives of peoples and nations.

History and sense of future intertwine to forge a consistent present and a space for meaningful identity. At the heart of that possibility of being which is man, we find the question of power and freedom radically posed.

From our perspective history is basically the source of man's transcendence. So, history does not essentially coalesce in the past but in the future which it projects (spiritual wealth, fullness of experience, strengthening of the sense of identity).

However, it might seem that philosophy is forbidden to answer the question of power and freedom with a look forward. Philosophy would be gibberish if it should pretend to guide us into the future.

The crisis of the narratives described by postmoderns and the dustbin to which the linguistic metaphilosphers relegate philosophical investigation confirm Hegel's dictum at the end of the preface to *The Principles of Philosophy of Right*: "The owl of Minerva spreads its wings only with the falling of the dusk."

The history of thought gives good reasons to describe the philosophical mission with this formula, so often repeated and seldom defined. But for us what matters is that it has achieved the status of paradigm for philosophical activity, even for declared adversaries of Hegelianism.

The formula's full force becomes apparent when it is seen as the culmination of a paragraph: "As the thought of the world, it appears only when actuality is already there cut and dried after its process of formation has been completed."[2] So, philosophy is admitted as "critical history," although it is incapable of thinking the future. In the last analysis, philosophy can be a systematic inventory which legitimates one bid for power to the detriment of another, a kind of "speculative tribunal," which only intellectually consummates the horizon of meaning in which man has developed a moment of his vocation for infinity, but which *does not accompany him in his full aspiration for it.*

Habermas explains that Hegel in *Philosophy of Right* thinks that: "Philosophy cannot instruct the world about how it ought to be; only reality as it is, is reflected in its concepts."[3] "It is no longer aimed critically against reality but against opaque abstractions wedged between subjective consciousness and the configurations of objective reason. After the spirit has struck its blow in modernity, after it has also found a way out of the aporias of modernity, and not only entered into reality but become objective in it, Hegel sees philosophy as absolved of the task of confronting with its concept the decadent existence of a social and political life. To this *blunting of critique* there corresponds a *devaluation of actuality*, from which the servants of philosophy turn away. Modernity, once brought to its concept, permits a stoic retreat from it."[4]

Hegel perceives the relation between modernity, time consciousness, and rationality, and is the first thinker for whom the modern period becomes a problem, indeed the fundamental problem of philosophy. Still, he cannot consider its self- affirmation, because in his intent to apprehend the modern period conceptually and thus to give an account of *his* time, he neglects to confront it as *possibility* as well. We understand that this is precisely what he cannot think because of his idea of philosophy as "tribunal" and—curiously and paradoxically—because philosophy is consumed by the understanding. He makes this clear in another important passage. Toward the end of *The Philosophy of Religion*, he remarks: " However the temporal, empirical present may find its way out of estrangement, however it may form itself, is to be left to it and is not an immediate, practical affair and concern of philosophy."[5]

The most rigorous disciples of Hegel also fail to appropriate this possibility of history itself for human aspiration, that is, its "futurity," because their model of modernity lacks this possibility. Neoconservative thinkers (right-wing Hegelians) have it still less. As Habermas correctly notes: "The party of Neoconservatives stemming from right Hegelianism yields uncritically to the rampaging dynamism of social modernity, in as much as it trivializes the modern consciousness of time, and prunes reason back into the understanding and rationality back into purposive rationality."[6] This description fits contemporary neoconservatism, some of whose aspects we will analyze in the present study.

Evidently, the majority of professional philosophers have not bothered to examine in depth the presumed universal validity or historical, normative consistency of that Hegelian dictum about philosophy. Nor have they even doubted about his diagnosis of the nature of philosophizing. Despite what has been written and thought about reason, we believe with Heidegger, that "calculating" thought, the domain of the understanding, constantly occupies the gaps in clarity of Western consciousness.

Yet, as we have written on several occasions, philosophy is a path open to truth and freedom. Therefore it is shaped in the critical movement of human freedom which depends on reason in its aspiration to attain a serene justification of the principles of life itself.[7] For us philosophy is not only consummation and legitimation of *facta*, of what has already been, as Hegel's phrase asserted. Rather, summing up the inquiry, it takes flight and penetrates into the sense of the future, without renouncing the historicity that is manifested in this modality of thought with a surprising intensity (which obviously does not always imply complete intelligibility). Philosophy cannot abandon its commitment to the finite, precisely because it is in its nature to have to accompany man in his aspiration to infinity. Thence its *problematic* character.[8] Its "business" is precisely the lacerations characteristic of finitude to avoid fleshless flights of thought.

2. The Question of Man

The previous section's distinction between what might be called "philosophies of legitimation" and "philosophies of hope" is fundamental in its conceptual implications. If philosophy practiced in the West was born as an aspiration to wisdom (hence, *philo-sophia*), as a path and not as possession, it obviously should focus on man and his possibilities rather than fixating on scholastic disputations about what has been, with no attempt to transcend circumstances of facts and more importantly of desire. Science, metaphysics, art, religion, and law are human possibilities. Consequently, the anthropological resonance of philosophical questions raised in each of them is inevitable since man is a totality.

In this sense, we have pointed out elsewhere that in the course of its history the consubstantiality of philosophical questions with the ultimate concerns of man has allowed that our discipline be exalted in rank with regard to the knowledge of science. Conversely, its weaknesses of finitude and impotence to effectively specify propositions capable of transforming the world have also been stressed. If the understanding opposes these emphases, on a different level, reason speaks to us about the unity between the human and the philosophical calling.[9] A fragment of Heraclitus, sums up our point eloquently: "Man ought to remember man, who forgets where the road leads." Accordingly, philosophical reason—not that understanding which only sees partially and schematically—will accompany man since the latter aspiration to infinity,[10] transcendence, and completion where his potentiality can be the fullest. But the discouragement inherent in such a quest will also accompany the search. It does not have definitive replies, characteristic of dogmatic, pseudoscientific knowledge, which would satiate human ontological, existential hunger.

This claim can be understood more completely if we distinguish between "problem" and "question." A problem is basically an obstacle to our contact with reality which has a solution insofar as we adopt an appropriate methodology and possess necessary information or knowledge. But a question like "What is man?," "What is life?," or "What is the world?" is a search for meaning. Properly speaking, philosophy deals with questions; with searches for meaning in other words, not problems. It is not a science in the positive acceptation, nor theology, although it is rigorous, systematic, intensive, and paradigmatically critical knowledge. The intellectual or practical solution—including the scientific or theological answer—does not finish a question, because any answer opens new dimensions of meaning significant for the searcher's existence. When this does not happen, we are in the presence of some form of veiling or masking of reality.

We recall Max Müller's penetrating observation:[11] "The measure of a philosophy, an art, a religion is not exactness but truth, 'depth,' the 'rank,' the 'level,' that is to say the intensity with which it sheds new light on the totality of meaning rather than the accurate grasp of a determined objective fact."

To deal with the question of man is finally to attend to his deepest existential concerns. The issue of power and freedom is found in our daily worries and in the most elementary or most elaborate human arrangements. Thus, there is no claim about meaning, even those that expressly deny validity to such claims, which does not suppose an answer to these questions. Evidently, when the philosophy of law reflects upon the future of man, it is closely tied to human projects and possibilities. It suffices to reflect on research into cloning[12]—practical results are expected by 2010—to ponder the importance of a nonideological approach to the question of man and the immense task which falls to the philosophers of law. Our investigation aspires to contribute some elements to this indispensable debate about man and his possibilities, situating the question of power and freedom and encouraging an interrogation open to the spiritual and moral advancement of humanity.

3. Our Working Hypothesis

The working hypothesis which guides our investigation is really a group of propositions which can be developed individually, but which are interdependent as regards the destiny of man. The destiny of man is considered here in anticipation of an eventual philosophy of law which could face the challenge of this question to think about the future with creative imagination, that is, with a kind of rationality which is not automatically self-limiting in its capacity for meaning.

To accomplish this task, we must get used to overcoming in our reflective practice the peculiar style of philosophizing typical of "tribunal speculation." Guidance comes from certain directives that inspired our criticism of that self-limiting Hegelian approach.

Proposition 1: Considered in general, power is an existential, and thus essentially informs human life.

Some preliminary clarifications can be made. The proposition is understood only if we situate the idea of power in a metaphysical or ontologico-existential plane, terms that are equivalent. Man is essentially power. In the first and most important analysis, it is not a question of the manifestations of power, of the different species of empirical social power. Without totally subscribing to Heidegger's thought, we have recourse to the term "existential" (*existenzial*), which already has a precise meaning in the history of philosophy; we wish to emphasize the specific constitutive character of power for man, precisely in virtue of its complement or counterpart in meaning, which is *freedom*. We are in the presence of a mode of being which is characteristically human. This level of analysis widens the epistemological basis of social science descriptions and explanations about the historical experience of man. Obviously, *analogies* can be established with other natural beings, but in all cases they will be illustrative.

Proposition 2: Power cannot be conceived without the idea of freedom.

Freedom and power are two aspects of the same reality. Both characterize man *ontologically*. Power is temporality, historical realization; and there is no historical realization without freedom. Our definition, or rather our defining approximation of man, can be understood completely in the light of these "existentials."[13] (We repeat that we use the term without adopting Heidegger's philosophy. The expression seems appropriate for our purposes because of its use in contemporary philosophical work, even with implications that might arise from some unforeseen further usage.) By way of an image, Proposition 2 states that freedom and power are the heads and tails of the same coin, without which there would be no coin. More traditionally, they can be assimilated to matter and form in Aristotelian substance.

Proposition 3: Power is objectification of freedom.

Power turns out to be the *objective* articulation of freedom with the world. The *subjective* articulation is freedom itself in its meaningful or sense-giving role. Accordingly, with his freedom and power man can make himself an object of alienation and destruction or else develop his lucidity,[14] that is, be the protagonist of a personal and communal destiny.

Proposition 4: Law is the regulation of power and freedom in a determined society according to a spirit of justice.

At first glance, that law is the regulation of power and freedom is not difficult to understand, if power and freedom are understood as "spaces of identity" that man acquires by his development as a person in relation with others. What is fundamental is the requirement that the regulation be carried out "according to a spirit of Justice." By "spirit of Justice" we understand the harmonic adjustment between spaces of freedom to which each man's characteristic moments of liberty and power tend, in the framework of a society as well as of each society with regard to other societies. Often this "spirit of Justice" did not exist or was partialized by being formalized as masking and in favor of a space of identity. (This has been the customary situation of mankind and hence of the superficial interpretation of power and freedom.) Then law comes to legitimate depersonalizing uses of power and the cancellation of individual and national freedoms.

Proposition 5: A reflection about the future of law in postmodern society is necessary.

Since the utopic version of modernity, that dystopia that has been called "postmodernity," has veiled power and freedom as human possibilities of being in their "spirit of Justice," it is clear that we need to commit ourselves to investigate the role and mode of existence of law in postmodern society.

This hypothesis admits:

1. A strong affirmation that the utopian project of modernity (ideal of man, reason, and society) emptied the notion of power of any content which was not directly or indirectly related to the idea of domination. Consequently, the realization of this power in science, and in society, was manifested as appropriation, subjection, and control.

Law and philosophy, with some exceptions, have legitimated this spiritual vocation of one part of humanity (the European part). For this it was necessary to universalize the character of one type of reason and its implicit axiology. This process facilitated the theoretical and practical justification of normalizing and subjugating all sectors of human activity and geography.

2. The space of freedom that man thought he was conquering was translated into spaces of identity structured from the outside. Their mode of affirmation in the world is that of possession, with a progressive evaporation of the other as a significant difference and as enriching one's own horizon of meaning.

3. The nature of any utopia necessarily implies the dialectical determination of its dystopia. In other words, the utopian elements which structure modernity's project, on being historically achieved, were converted into dystopia. This new *topos* called postmodernity does not go beyond modernity, but, so to speak, is its earthly counterpart.

4. If, as we believe, our interpretation is consistent, law ought to reconsider the grounds of its normative output and whether it is proper to continue with schemes that seek legitimation either a priori (naturalism) or a posteriori (positivism).

Notes

1. Cicero, *De Conjuratione Catilinae*, 52, 21.

2. *Hegel's Philosoophy of Right*, trans. with notes by T. M. Knox (Oxford: Oxford University Press, 1945, 1958), 30.

3. Jürgen Habermas, *The Philosphical Discourse of Modernity, Twelve Lectures*, trans. Frederick G. Lawrence (Cambridge, Mass.: MIT Press, 1987, 1996) , 43.

4. Habermas, *Philosophical Discourse of Modernity*, 43.

5. Quoted by Habermas, *Philosophical Discourse of Modernity*, 36, from G. W. F. Hegel, *The Christian Religion: Lectures on the Philosophy of Religion*, Part III, *The Revelatory Consummate, Absolute Religion* (Missoula, Mont.: Scholars Press, 1979), 297.

6. Habermas, *Philosophical Discourse of Modernity*. 43.

7. See especially chapters 2 and 3 in the present work and H. Daniel Dei, "Situación de la Filosofía del Derecho en la Sociedad Postmoderna," in *Actas de las V Jornadas Argentinas de Filosofía Jurídica y Social*, Mar del Plata, April 4-6, 1989.

8. On philosophy as discipline of problematic knowledge, see Niccola Abbagnano, *Filosofía, Religión, Ciencia* (Buenos Aires: Editorial Nova, 1961). Also, see Plato, *Symposium* 204 a-c on the role of love as an intermediate nature in relation to philosophy.

9. See chapter 2, section 1, of the present work.

10. As a first conceptual approximation, we said, "man is a finite being with aspirations of infinity," in our study, "Conciencia de catástrofe, poder y libertad," in II Congreso Internacional de Filosofia del Derecho, Plata, May 19-23, 1987, vol. 1, 27-37; an expanded version of this paper appeared in 399-405 of *Revista de Filosofía de la Universidad de Costa Rica*, volume 27, no. 66, 1989, especially 401. Our essay "La cuestión del hombre" will develop the philosophical implications of this statement, and in a way, synthesize line of thought initially sketched in *Bases para una Antropodicea*.

11. Max Müller, *Crisis de la Metafísica*, trans. A. Klein (Buenos Aires: Editorial Sur, 1962), 154.

12. When the Spanish version of the present work was in press, *The New York Times* published the news, already familiar to specialists, that researchers at the George Washington University Laboratory of Fertilization *in vitro* had accomplished the first positive results in an experiment in cloning a human being. News reports declared that those in charge of the experiment halted work to establish "ethical guidelines." As presented by the wire services, the odd justification of Laboratory Director Robert Stillman seems more a legal precaution than a deliberate assumption of an ethical code for science: "This has been a way of avoiding ethical controversy. We are looking for directives which will indicate whether this is the right path or not." By such affirmations the scientist is only an employee of political and technological interests. This is far removed from the ideas of Albert Einstein, J. Dausset, I. Prigogine, and many others, about scientists' moral responsibility.

13. See note 10 of this chapter.

14. By "lucidity," as used above, José Isaacson refers to the process of "desalienation." In his words, "the person is the project which an individual assumes when he opts for lucidity, that is, for disalienation. Hence individual and person are limit states, the first of which marks man as member of a species, and the second as a person analogous to the divine person, or in secular terms, as disalienated man. An individual oscillates between these limits and must be considered a project." *Antropología literaria*, (Buenos Aires: Marymar, 1982, 1. Cf. also Isaacson's *La Revolución en la Persona* (Buenos Aires: Marymar, 1980), 17 ff.

Chapter 6

Metaphysics of Power

1. Methodological Foundations of Our Discourse

The model commonly used in the social sciences interprets power as external, as a network of specific psychosocial bonds. Further, when a thinker formed in the social sciences refers to "metaphysical foundations," he usually identifies confusedly—and wrongly—what is strictly metaphysical with what is mythical, religious, or supernatural. However nuanced, even in the case of neo-Thomist realism, this model follows the basic argument of historic positivism, whose intellectualist rationalism impedes any understanding of power in existential terms.

For a number of reasons we reject this kind of interpretation, at least in its globalizing and philosophical pretensions. These interpretations are epistemologically self-limiting and ultimately acritical. They flatten the planes on which the phenomenon that concerns us may be approached. Among other, more complex, philosophical presuppositions, these interpretations do not distinguish power, considered in itself, generically, from its empirical manifestations. Consequently, in their historical, political exposition they explain externally both a determined order's legitimating devices as well as the source of legitimacy for the acts of power.

Accordingly, philosophical inquiries about the essence of this phenomenon cannot be entirely situated within the framework of empirical or situational analyses of historical events. At present certain multidisciplinary, cybernetic approaches undertake the task.[1] The Argentine social researcher Labourdette warns[2] us about the implicit mechanism at work in certain theories of power which explain aspects of human behavior. Labourdette claims that these approaches "from an explicit commitment to employ a theoretical apparatus whose mainstay is the concept of power inappropriately extrapolate to the empirical and specifically to a commitment by way of postures and actions of power, especially political ones." In the end this mechanism reduces the very concept "to identify it with one of its aspects: coercion, repression, physical imposition, force, etc."

To be sure, "power impregnates the social edifice much more than is ordinarily perceived or scientifically described; it is mixed with other things and sometimes hidden." In this vein, J. C. Smith's useful distinction[3] specifies that what we call "power" should more properly be called "social power." When the social sciences speak of religious, political, juridical power, and so on, they simply refer to different species of social power. Even with such methodological reservations about the positive stage of analysis of power, to our way of thinking, the most refined methods of the positive science cannot reveal what power *essentially* is, because these sciences cannot go beyond causal, or even genetic, functional analyses. They will always be limited by a context of interpretation for which they cannot account. In the field of law, an example of these difficulties of grounding was the unsuccessful, although painstaking, effort of Carlos S. Nino to explain the concept of human rights.[4]

Philosophically speaking, we believe that the reflection about this question—not this problem, let us recall—admits another level of analysis, from which this question can enrich the positive approaches without necessarily invalidating them. The ground of the phenomenon of power can thus be understood; the modality of its projection into all human activities can be clarified; and the sociopolitical research can be endowed with an existential, phenomenological approach which is less colored by a priori ideological assumptions and closer to the fundamental structure of existence.

We adopt this higher level of analysis methodically; it situates our subject in the specific metaphysical context, as announced in the explanation of the first proposition in our working hypotheses.

The mere mention of a metaphysical approach can awaken antagonisms in the academic world or visceral rejection by "practical realists." We cannot offer remedies here for the personal aspects of this rejection, but it may also reflect failure to fully evaluate the exhaustion of the great speculative idealist systems as well as of the pretendedly scientific objective substitutes that followed them. What Heimsoeth denominates "methodological crisis"[5] became particularly acute in the second half of the nineteenth century for "intrinsic, objective, reasons" (historical) and because of the earlier decisive push from Kantian criticism, which to our thinking, reappears less subtlely in subsequent thought. Thus, with the exception of the efforts of thinkers like Max Scheler and above all the vast work of Heidegger, philosophers abdicated from "the aspirations of metaphysics to take over a deductive character that is purely aprioristic and system-wide apodictic certainty."[6] Once its sources as *prima philosophia* have been left behind, this sort of (dogmatic) metaphysics seemed crudely at the margin of the questions of being and existence and ultimately incapable of responding to the renewed human requirements of meaning. The positive sciences took its place. They "changed their course toward the empirical, the hypothetical, the relative, what could always be revised even in its principles."

Echoing the utilitarian rationality of the industrial revolution, "positivism (Comte, Laas, Mach, Avenarius, and others) demands complete abandonment of metaphysics, that it abdicate in favor of positive sciences and their work upon natural experience. . . . Metaphysical problems are rejected with a mien of scientific gravity, as pseudo-scientific, falsely posed, perturbing scientific progress." Positivism decrees that "the efforts of metaphysics should be counted as part of the dead past of a humanity now entered into science, just like the religious and mythological products of the fantasy of far away periods."[7]

With this partial understanding,[8] the neo-Kantian movement (Cohen, Natorp, and Riehl, among others) lost the point of Kantian criticism and turned against metaphysics. Using the model of social sciences and their results, it aspires to measure the value of philosophical propositions.[9]

In this context the inevitable next step becomes the approach to philosophy as "rigorous science." Despite his intent, Edmund Husserl's formidable critical effort could not entirely avoid the influence of dominant scientism.

We agree with Heimsoeth's view that these philosophical tendencies "are far from being as free from metaphysics as they think." One could add that the healthy opposition to dogmatism in one area of knowledge cannot consistently legitimate it in another. Although this sounds obvious, it is a truth seldom heeded in human history.

The metaphysical approach we propose precludes any attempt to rejuvenate a kind of knowledge of the absolute and the "suprasensible." Nothing would distort our central point more, since we build precisely upon the complete acceptance of man's finite situation. As we see it, the connection of power and freedom with man's ontological, existential structure, his *metaphysical nature*, opens the possibility of a fertile comprehension of his manner of *being* and *acting* in the world. Hence we reaffirm that authentic metaphysical thought (and authentic philosophical thought in any epoch) is not a "speculation," or in a more popular interpretation, the usual evasion or interested justification of an established power, at least not in its original purpose. This holds against both those who still pontificate in the name of dogmatic metaphysics as well as those who defend a concept of world, man, and being in general as militant anti-metaphysicians. What is more, "When Western metaphysics is really great, it always thinks against itself and against representability and objectivity. It is at the same time permanent rebellion against itself and this anti-metaphysical thought (Gegendenken) necessarily belongs to metaphysical thought of authentic degree."[10] Therefore, fossilized metaphysical philosophisms falsify any reflection and stray from the path of communication in the same way as implicit metaphysical messages which support pretendedly scientific considerations. *Authentic* metaphysical reflection constantly redefines its intentions and is nourished by the inquiry itself, because (a) it consists of "questions" and (b) it is the highest *rational* mode in which man confronts the radical themes of his existence.[11]

On this higher level of analysis, the questions here considered transcend sociopolitical positions, which does not mean that we are ethically neutral. Besides, it seems methodologically adequate to situate power first where it is essentially constituted as a source of possible meanings, logically prior to the diverse phenomenal modalities of which the social sciences give an account.

2. The Sources of Power: Finitude and Freedom

Where is power essentially constituted as a source of possible meanings?

Indisputably, power is a source of meaning for man. What is less clear is why this notion functions as the principle of social relations. Our thesis does not permit us to conceive power as the *theoretical point of departure* from which explanations about human interaction follow. Power may be "present in the most subtle mechanisms" of social life, and even if not everything is still "everywhere," as Foucault says, who is acknowledged to have articulated the most important account of power circulating in the academic world. Still, that would not justify its being the source of meaning. The definitions of power which describe its defects are not satisfactory. Definitions conceived in this way are vitiated by the partiality of our reference point and our interests. Only when we discover *where* power is properly, essentially constituted, can we understand its meaningful dimension for human existence. Since our definition attempts to face the question of what power is, beyond its many and varied empirical manifestations, we ask about the source, the *topos* in which it is constituted as of mode of being of existence.

Consequently, our thesis affirms that the sources of power are freedom as possibility of signifying a world, an order of sense, and finitude as the characteristic mode of human existence, insofar as power is the specific capacity for spatiotemporal determinations of the possibilities of freedom. The concretion of liberty is power. To affirm that power is a source of meanings for man is to say that power unfolds the order of meaning configured by freedom. From this viewpoint, power loses the character of a phantasm which informs everything and to which everything seems to be submitted. It is revealed as an *existential*, a constitutive element of the very being of human existence.

Two thinkers recognized for their contribution to this theme, Bertrand de Jouvenel and Michel Foucault, deserve special mention as prototypes of the approach to social science. They allow us to illustrate our point of view critically. For de Jouvenel, to speak of the source of power is to speak of the *topos* from which authority is legalized and legitimated, the question of the essence of power is practically settled within the limits of the discussion of sovereignty, in the framework of an identification of power with political power. For Foucault, this problematic hides the relations of forces at play beneath the efforts at justification, so that he extends the notion of power to the multiple relations that are formed and operate in the social body.

Let us start with a reflection offered in Bertrand de Jouvenel's classic, *On Power*.[12] Ever since Aristotle's *Politics* reduced political structures of different societies "to three basic types: monarchy, aristocracy, and democracy . . . [T]he characteristics of these three types, in the various mixtures in which they are found in practice, accounted for all the forms of Power which had come under his observation. . . . Ever since then political science, or what passes for such, has followed obediently in the footsteps of the master. The discussion of the different forms of Power is always with us because, there being in every society a center of control, everyone is naturally interested in the question of its powers, its organization, and its conduct." De Jouvenel adds the point we wish to stress: "There is, however, another phenomenon that also deserves some consideration: the fact that over every human community there reigns a government at all. The differences between forms of government and different societies and the changes of form within the same society are but the accidents, to borrow the terminology of philosophy, of one and the same essence. The essence is Power. And we may well break off from inquiring into *what is the best form of Power*—in political ethics—to ask *what is the essence of Power*—in order to construct a political metaphysic."

Whether we look at the problem from the exercise of command or, as de Jouvenel himself subsequently suggests, from obedience, he undermines his declared intention to know the meaning of power when he says that (1) it implies the constitution of a political metaphysics, a formulation which rests on the assumption that power is identified with one of its species, and (2) the object of his investigation "in reality and speaking *grosso modo*, are the relations between power and society," which confirms the existence of the assumption just noted.

Of course, to ask about the essence of power cannot lead to an appropriate platform for analysis on de Jouvenel's path. Obviously, this type of inquiry calls for a noninstrumental reply. The deviation of a thinker of Bertrand de Jouvenel's stature from the inquiry provoked by his observation, "that a government exists in every human group," confirms what we have previously said about the epistemological difficulty of the positive sciences taking charge of the real implications of asking about what power essentially is.

We could almost say that with this inquiry, the history of political and legal thought has entered the well-plowed field of the concept of sovereignty. Behind sovereignty are at stake the problems of both legality and legitimacy of authority, that is, of whoever exercises power. It is not an accident that the idea of power has been traditionally identified with that of authority.

De Jouvenel insists that even "theories like those of Divine Right and Popular Sovereignty, which pass for opposites, stem in reality from the same trunk, the idea of sovereignty—the idea, that is, that somewhere there is a right to which all other rights must yield. It is not hard to discover behind this juridical concept a metaphysical one. A supreme will, it runs, rules and disposes human societies, a Will, which being naturally good, it would be wrong to resist, a will that is either the 'Divine Will' or the 'general will.'"[13]

We can go still further with the real meaning of this fundamental politico-legal category. Historically, law has tried to explain its necessary connection with power, and also establish its difference. But it would seem that it can only ratify facts of power with a normative order. This is what Kelsen's fundamental norm does in a way.[14] For the moment, let us omit other observations which might be made, because we would like to stress an aspect which concerns us more directly. We believe that the idea of sovereignty, and more precisely, that of *sovereign power*, eloquently illustrates the existential character of power. If we abandon the formal academic history of this concept, we will note that the discourse has covered the justification or the limitation of the possession of normative power, the capacity to modify rules of behavior imposed on subjects or to define the norms which preside over the one's own action. In the last analysis we have looked at the justification, if possible, of legislative power over the laws themselves[15] and sanctioned by God himself. This is only one more perspective in the multifaceted aspiration to omnipotence which summons us frequently when we want to placate the consciousness of finitude. Reason or, better, more or less inspired rationalizations have served us as a club to feed the fantasies of metaphysical security.

In the tension between justification and limitation of a space of freedom assured by the supposed possession of legislative power, law implodes as regulatory possibility and with it the value of justice. What is just and unjust, morally right or appropriate, does not seem to be derived by asking about the question of man and about his effective ontological, existential posture, if we must restrict ourselves to bookish history, sanitized of more profound passions and sentiments.

Michel Foucault is a genuine product of French intellectualism who has subtly nourished European ethnocentrist rationalism. He, too, concerns himself with the idea of sovereignty.[16] With a strong dose of argumentative ambiguity and with gestures to the gallery of his interlocutors (gestures of power), he poses the relation between power, law, and truth: "My problem is rather this: what rules of right are implemented by the relation of power in the production of discourses of truth?" He adds what he takes to be an equivalent question: "Or alternatively, what type of power is susceptible of producing discourses of truth that in a society such as ours are endowed with such potent effects?" Next, he broadens the understanding of his questions by explaining: "What I mean is this: in a society such as ours, but basically in any society, there are manifold relations of power which permeate, characterize, and constitute the social body, and these relations of power cannot themselves be established, consolidated, or implemented without the production, accumulation, circulation, and functioning of a discourse. There can be no possible exercise of power without a certain economy of discourses of truth which operates through and on the basis of this association. We are subjected to the production of truth through power, and we cannot exercise power except through the production of truth. This is the case for every society, but I believe that in ours the relationship between power, right, and truth is organized in a highly specific fashion." For Foucault, legal thought, especially about royal sovereign power, has developed this special mode of relation between law and power since the Middle Ages; conceptually, the whole theory of law is organized around the problem of sovereignty. In this conclusion, Foucault does not differ from Bertrand de Jouvenel or any other historian of law.

But does the text cited say more? Let us look more closely. When we read the original statement of the problem which gives rise to his reflections, we observe that the subject of the issue is relations of power. That subject is none other than the social body since these relations are what characterize and constitute it. With less ambiguity, the proposition would be: the relations of power (or the social body) are functionalized, circulated, and so on, by the rules of law through the production of a discourse of truth (that is, rationalizations that legitimate, sustain, and above all, keep feeding the relations of power). Does this not set the stage for a discussion of the old sociological theme of social control?

In reality, what Foucault means is that in every society and especially in Western society there is a "model" (which we would call European) of production of truth. Logically, he next makes a complementary inquiry regarding causality, which would *seem* to indicate that law is a type of power capable of producing discourses of truth. (Let us deliberately set aside at this point a criticism of what the author refers to as "truth" and consider the word only in what we take to be the restricted use of "legitimating discourse.") Properly speaking, Foucault does not clarify or clarifies insufficiently what he means by "power" in the inquiry, even less why he alters the character of the initial investigation. Equivocation in the use of the word "power" is precisely what gives his argument its impact. According to the passage quoted and in Foucault's work generally, power is diffused in the very weave of society but ultimately has a place and a name, the sovereign, the authority, whomever circumstances give possession of force or *capacity of domination.*

Behind his whole inquiry is the idea of "sovereignty." However, the text and imprecise subsequent explanations suggest a connection which is logical rather than factual between this idea, law, and what could be summed up as "authority," objectified sometimes in the figure of the king and other times in that of the bourgeoisie or the state. In a less subtle analysis, it is clear that Foucault's proposal affirms that the instrument which grounds his model of production of truth and implementation of power is law. In the West, this is accomplished by means of the reconstitution of the juridical structure and reactivation of Roman Law after the Middle Ages. This law is a "law directed by the king." Its principal objective is to "fix the legitimacy of power." Whatever the discussions that continue to be provoked by the problem of sovereignty, the problem is centered on this point, which allows us to understand the nature of political power but not the very essence of power. A further observation may be made. We do not believe that the problem here is that power masks itself to facilitate its intentions, as Foucault seems to suggest. Any organized human group offers difficulties of this type. Although this law can be seen as an instrument, it tries also to regulate its effects from many different points of view. This cannot be evaded in any serious historical investigation. So the following claim about masking seems unilateral and even self-contradictory to us: "When we say that sovereignty is the central problem of right in Western society, what we mean basically is that the essential function of the discourse and technique of right has been to efface the domination intrinsic to power in order to present the latter at the level of appearance under two different aspects: on the one hand as the legitimate rights of sovereignty, and on the other, as the legal obligation to obey it. The system of right is entirely centered upon the king, and it is therefore designed to eliminate the fact of domination and its consequences."[17]

For us, both domination and submission are results of a wrongly understood concept of power. The rights invoked by the dominator will inevitably take the form of a kind of rationality to support his position, objectified in more or less elaborate norms and rules of law. But this does not "efface the domination intrinsic to power," since domination—all domination—dissolves power and submits it to whoever exercises it. It is therefore obliged to produce eternal discourses of truth and extend control even further than the law. Psychology might label this a kind of repetition compulsion based on the fear—well grounded—of losing power. It is not by accident that the bourgeoisie details procedures of social marginalization even more minutely than royal power. The bit of explanation of this phenomenon attempted by Foucault is limited by his approach (which we could say corresponds to the "micromechanics" of bourgeois interest). It is thus not a question of avoiding the question of sovereignty and in its place "to substitute the problem of domination and submission for that of sovereignty and obedience."[18] Even when we liberate ourselves from this idea in search of a "nondisciplinary power" and we aspire to articulate "antidisciplinarian" law, something which alludes to the question itself will subsist in still more sophisticated forms.[19] The harshness of the methodological perspective posed in terms of thought like Foucault's does not stimulate lucidity about the phenomenon, but rather refurbishes old ideologies, and encourages a new and finer mechanism of domination in those who hold power. On the contrary, we believe it necessary to entirely assume the character of a question that seems to underlie the theme. For that we need to return to the query posed by Bertrand de Jouvenel and left without an answer about the very essence of power. Indeed the question of sovereignty summons us to inquire about just that, if we abandon the shallow waters washed over by the social sciences.

To ask about the essence of power is to ask about its *nature*. Thus the search can only direct us to what makes power exist. Beyond any discussion, it is necessary to discover what is its specific determination. For that, it is not enough to clarify the use of the term, because in that case power in itself would continue to be a gap of unintelligibility which relativizes the comprehension of the phenomena where it is manifested. However, when we ask about the essence of power, about its nature, we obviously ask about the intrinsic *principle* (*arché*) of power.

At the beginning of Book Delta of the *Metaphysics* (1012b lines 35 ff), Aristotle affirms that every principle has a common trait, present in acceptations and modes of which it is regarded as the principle. This trait is to be the first *from which* (*hothen*) something is, is generated, and is known. Applied to our topic, "from which" remits us to the source in which power finds its specific determination, its proper being. This source from which power arises as possibility of meanings for man is the radically finite, contingent character of our ontological, existential structure. In other words, *power is essentially constituted in the finitude of our existence and in the necessity of unfolding our liberty*. This approach to the question situates us on a level of analysis which avoids giving preferential treatment to any of the figures in which power is expressed in history, and reveals to us the very condition of its being. Contrary to what we might suppose, the idea of power alludes to ontological lack in man, to his need for completion, and corresponds to that aspiration to infinitude of his freedom which defies the tragic consciousness of nothingness that we also are.

If we recur to anthropological data from the study of religion, power can be better understood as a specifically human mode of being. But it is necessary to reflect critically on traditional hermeneutical paradigms of power. This is so for two reasons. On the one hand, we think of power as an attribute of divinity; on the other hand, when we identify it with efficacy (a charge of power) of persons, objects, places, or actions, phenomena customarily denominated taboo, mana, or by analogous terms in different cultures. Thus, for example, when we speak of the "power of God," we really want the expression to reflect the perfect plenitude of God's being. But being and power are not the same. The difference is the abyss and incomparable ontological distance between God and man. *What Is* eminently is not subject to the forced change implicit in the idea of power. The religious person of every period has sought to narrow this gap, "saturating himself with being" by his participation of sacred time and space. Let us agree that "God is powerful" is a manner of speaking about a reality which imposes itself and awes us by its mere presence, because speaking with propriety, God *is*. To need power to be is an unavoidably finite condition. We believe that only an abusively anthropocentric use of language lets us affirm that He who "has" Being, must also have Power. This connection is necessary only for the person who extrapolates and ontifies as a superlative term what constitutes the possibilities of historical realization of his existence. It is now possible to have a complete perspective on our affirmation that the theme of sovereignty remits to a question which surpasses the positive type of analysis to which social sciences are epistemologically tied. This is the reason why both Bertrand de Jouvenel and Michel Foucault can only reveal facets in which power is manifested in society.

Thus, to affirm that power is an existential and that it informs the life of man essentially, as we proposed in the first of our hypotheses, is to refer the meaning of power to the ontological structure of existence.

3. Characterization of Power

The expression "power" carries a burden of conceptual vagueness like few others. It has intrinsic and acquired, affective and intellectual resonances. The word names capacities, processes, and aspirations as well as the goal and culmination of an action. It even sets itself up as a value per se, a reference point to consolidate the identity of an individual or social group of whatever extension. It is also perceived as a criterion to measure the consistency of a symbolic or real entity.

However, as we already said, the idea of power is almost always restricted to the sociopolitical realm and, consequently, is understood only in relation to this type of phenomena. An old controversy between power and liberty continues to transfix the elements of the problem. Natural components of social life appear as competitors for political spaces, lived as spaces of identity which represent greater or lesser levels of freedom of power. Examples of what we say can be observed in the authors discussed in section 2 of this chapter, most transparently in Bertrand de Jouvenel's *On Power*.[20] The work is an eloquent exposition of this rivalry: rivalry between power embodied in some institutional figure like the State or the Sovereign and individual liberty. Another example is the liberal ideological mystique which sees the dynamic of its historical analysis in this opposition. Historians generally disguise this interpretation as an objective perception or observation of social reality.[21] The interpretation leads us to think of freedom negatively as mere resistance in the general scheme of possible zones of activity or of individual rights possessed by members of a particular society.

Surely, this way of conceiving freedom limits the impact of a key tool for the comprehension of man. Paradoxically, freedom is a constitutive anthropological concept. Its richness and universality have both the greatest comprehension, encompassing essential characteristics of the human species, as well as the greatest extension, since it is applicable to every individual human. Its resonances apply both diachronically and synchronically, enveloping every possible human experience. So we claim that freedom is not only a characteristic human faculty among others, but that it is also the possibility of meaningful unity of which the concretion (*concrescere*) of the whole imaginative human world consists, whether understood as closed or open to transcendence.[22]

Obviously, in our immediate consciousness, power and liberty are linked to their historical embodiments. But it is also obvious that there is an interpretative leap in the tendency to consider their manifestations as perfected achievements of power and liberty in themselves, without considering that they are all immersed in the contingency proper to the temporality in which they take place. Our effort is precisely to ascend from the datum to the concept which grounds the intelligibility of these phenomena, where we discover the peculiar ontological structure revealing the deepest sense of the positive achievements of power and liberty.

In regard to the last point, it must be specified that civil liberties and even political liberties are mere social epiphenomena when they are not grounded in a participated, comprehensive horizon of meaning, which frames them as necessary corollaries within the social practice which each community lives as a nuclear bond. These particular liberties are some of the ways according to which it is usual to regulate power in contemporary societies. Instead of exhausting their meanings as variables which characterize the social order, they show their full efficacy in developing the person—and his lucidity as a citizen—if they maintain a close correspondence to an internalized conception of world and life. An internalized conception has an informal worldview, not foreign to the real history of the people which accepts these freedoms as part of their social dynamic. By contrast, in the experience of many nations, as is logical, these liberties are often open to excesses, deviations, or violations, exactly because of the lack of an adequate ontological support and a coherent psychosocial and legal backing.

So, we affirm that power ontologically considered is not fatally determined to be corrupting or oppressive. It is in the actualization of freedom, the act by which we appropriate a world meaningfully, where power finds the possibilities of being constituted as promoter of an integrating sense for man and the community to which he belongs or else he may become an independent agent. In the latter case, the configuration of the aspiration toward totality and permanence which moves man is transformed ipso facto into an infinity corroded by explicit or hidden contingency.

Despite empirical support for these assertions, our concepts would be insufficiently clear unless we accentuated the necessity of dialectical correlation between liberty and power, since power cannot be conceived without liberty (Proposition 2). Thus, if liberty is the possibility that man has of giving meaning to a world, an order appropriate for him from which he can understand himself, man sets this in motion and achieves it by power.[23] In a single uninterrupted, continuous movement of the spirit, the exercise of freedom and the consequent unfolding of power introduce the construction of a meaningful universe within which man recognizes himself and is understood. With it he seeks to overcome the tension of instability and uncertainty of his finite reality. He discovers, interprets, and accomplishes his particular life according to this meaning, and accepts it in his desires and emotions, in his internal states, and in the intentionality of his acts.

This explains why we say liberty and power are ontological constituents of his existence. That man is capable of struggling, suffering, and dying for them reveals that they are signs of his aspiration to infinity, of his contemplative longing, and of spaces of personal or group identity. By them he recognizes himself as a possibility of being and of belonging to a world.

The problem, then, is to know whether the experience of freedom and the accomplishments of his power are effectively directed to the fullness of his being, and consequently to the resolution of tension between his metaphysically finite nature and his vocation of infinity, or whether they deepen the uneasiness of nothingness, or pure contingency. In other words, we must explain how power is articulated with liberty, since power is its objectification (Proposition 3).

4. Levels of Manifestation of Power

When we speak of "levels of manifestation of power" we think of the modes in which power objectifies the actualization of freedom in time and space, and therefore how power acquires the different configurations in which it is usually conceived. If, as we said, finitude is the source of power's existentiality and its contingent character, freedom is the source of the positive determinations of power in history. This means there is a formal and material continuity between the experience of man's exercise of freedom and crystallizations of the meaning of power. This experience of freedom is found in activities and in culture (within which we include social forms). They are products of the exercise of freedom. However, in his aspiration to fullness man can configure the world from either ontological freedom (analogous to Augustine's *libertas*) or from psychological freedom (usually known as free choice). The meaning of his own existence is attained therein. But, besieged by his metaphysical poverty, man primarily seeks to achieve his aspirations of being in immediate empirical reality. By this he expects he can assure a space of identity, in the conviction that more possession of instruments of domination and dissuasion strengthen his presence in the world and confer necessity on the symbolic universe which sustains his acts. The peculiar mode of his relations with things, his dependence on tangible and intangible goods, and the segmental links with other humans, whether accidental or impersonal, soon ends by changing the meaning of his own perception of reality. Finally, that mode takes itself as an instrument in its desire to manipulate eternity for itself in the contingency of being.

Certain thematizations of this human aspiration like Schopenhauer's "will to live" or Nietzsche's "will to power" are only equivalent to the "will to domination" in the context of restricted freedom. The will to domination is naturally objectified as the settling, fixation, detention, and death of any *élan vital*, since its only goal and measure are its own struggle to impose itself upon the slavery of its eternal movement. There is nothing in the positive order which absolutely guarantees a space of identity. The challenge of everyday existence, of life and death, is slowly suffocated by psychological interventions of the freedom of possession and of power to dominate. Both create the illusion of permanence represented by circumstantial security, and lull disturbances provoked by finitude when consciousness raises its head. But, when the fear for the space just won is quieted, other spaces of identity rise up to make us doubt about our security, since the liberty of possession which is the source of this movement is sustained in pure contingency. Even formal external controls, imposed by a strong group or a juridically organized society to balance these tensions, do not suffice. For the aspirations to infinity and spaces of identity are not consolidated when power grasps instruments and makes them ultimate values. In this way, power becomes oppressive. It moves relations of submission even for those who seem to be masters of the risk and capable of great autonomy, because all their achievements are directed to protect the frontiers of the identity of being thus acquired. Then, autonomy and risk in freedom, which impel us to a bit of lucidity, are fenced in to guarantee security, quiet, and uniformity. Finally, the awareness of possible death can often rob the spontaneity of life, and the aspiration to transcendence and infinitude which mobilized the will to be fully feels itself harassed by the proximity of destruction, by loss, and nothingness as the only horizon of meaning.

A correlation between freedom and power as aspects of the same reality, man, affirms itself in the correspondence of meaning which exists between the constitutive act of freedom and the concretions of power. This explains the distinction we have been making between what might be called "power to be" and "power to dominate," grounded respectively in exercise of liberty on a different level (one metaphysical, the other psychological).[24]

A good example of this is the second mode in which power is manifested, which is precisely the object of the social sciences, in the customary practice of relations between states. In his useful work *The Relations of Nations*,[25] Frederick H. Hartmann describes how states view the problem of power in relation to their security and vital interest:

"Since states vary enormously in their power (i.e. in their ability in the last analysis to use force), the restraining effect, or lack of one, of the security arrangements of states varies roughly with the power of the states concerned." (In a footnote Hartmann elaborates: "It varies 'roughly' with the power of the states concerned because other states may perceive the power relationship erroneously or judge falsely the capability of one or more states to bring that power to bear effectively.") "It is relatively easy for a medium power to counter the ambitions of Guatemala, but it is extremely difficult for it to do the same things in terms of the United States or the Soviet Union. Nevertheless, while the restraint or lack of restraint depends upon the power of those to be restrained versus the power of the restrainers, and while states may be engaged in attempting either to maintain or overthrow an existing *status quo, no state can ignore the problem that confronts it as a result of the existence of other potentially hostile states.* In this respect all states are equal, for every one of them has a *power problem* that it must somehow resolve. That the particular nature of the problem will vary from state to state is important. That each state has a power problem is fundamental. The power problems of states are always at the core of their international relations. How each state conceptualizes its power problem will in turn determine its choices of national strategies designed to ensure national security [vital interests]."[26]

Before commenting on Hartmann, it is worth expanding on what he understands by power:

"Power, as we briefly defined the term . . . , means: How strong or weak is a given state? In a more formal sense, power is the strength or capacity that a sovereign nation-state can use to achieve its interests. . . . In this sense, the relations of sovereign states, each possessed of power, are always at root those of 'power politics.' Power that may be used is already being used, even though no overt or willful act by the state possessing that power has occurred."[27] When we refer to power used in the latter way, we call it *influence.*

According to Hartmann, the common factor in the relations between states is the type of power we have called "domination." More detailed analysis brings out other elements which provide reasons that support our theory and which it seems important to consider:

1. Each state has a problem of power as does each man, since it must achieve its identity. Willing or not, it must live in determined historical circumstances.

2. The corollary is that we cannot elude being in the world in some way. Therefore, in the example, the *"politics of power" for a state is closely related to the exercise of its freedom to be, to posit itself as a possibility,* here, we are at the limits between the metaphysical level (the sense of power) and the level of fact (how power operates). We see that both in states and organizations, which are human creations after all, the relation between the what and the how is necessary and direct, and that both *project and realization condition each other mutually.*

3. Therefore, the mode of resolution of power problem—in Hartmann's phrase—which includes lack of resolution as an alternative, depends for us on the taking of power, addition or subtraction of factors, whatever they may be, that intervene in the equation of power. Therefore, the manner in which each state conceives its problem of power is relevant.

4. But the problem of power which every state has is not resolved via the increase of material capacity of power but in *the capacity to situate itself at the*

level of the conception of freedom which it wants for itself, in its will to be. In turn that will determine the choice of means appropriate to its vocation, both strategic and operational, in all spheres of national life.

5. These means are strengthened precisely when they are nourished by a vocation to be which is felt by and rooted in all the members of a society; more exactly, in a freedom to be, and not to have, a power to be, and not to dominate.

6. In other words, it is not sufficient for power to be conferred legally, in a positive, visible form. The legitimacy of its presence must also conform to a true (effective) national image which is its will to be (metaphysical freedom) and for which power is just its historical expression. The harmonic synthesis of the terms of this resolution allow the problem of power to be satisfactorily resolved, as well as to better evaluate the relations of power of another state.

7. Otherwise, the power to dominate, grounded in an act of psychological freedom, makes having and possessing into the modalities of its aspiration to travel the path towards identity. By nature of its constitution this aspiration is a never-ending race. This type of affirmation of being is pursued only on the basis of what was conceived as an instrument, a means. This has consequences in social and political practices. "The instrumentalization of man—and of nations—by man, contributes to conflict and destruction," since the character of all violence is implicit in the historical choice that produces and reproduces it.[28]

Power to dominate inevitably brings the inversion of values and progressive lack of personal and community autonomy through a growing dependence on new totalitarian forms of social control. This facet, which a phenomenology of power makes evident, reaches its climax when we analyze the impact of the finitude-infinitude tension on another, more dramatic, international example. The use of atomic energy in war confronts humanity with the possible step of conceiving its absolute employment in world relations. The end of the cold war may be only a moment toward more unstable and violent different forms. The Gulf War is a symptom. We are certainly passing from the threat of partial destruction to unlimited intimidation. The possibility of being of some nations has become incredibly infinite, planetary: aspiration to national or regional transcendence seems to feed on domination and possession of a nuclear arsenal. Being fully and conserving identity is more than ever the result of the action of freedom of having and power of domination. This mentality justifies thinking that the guarantee of rationality in international relations is dissuasion by whoever possesses the absolute weapon, and by differentiated, hierarchical spaces of identity, like those in a firmly stratified society. From a different approach, Robert G. Wesson[29] affirms: "Under modern conditions the chief cause of conflict is the demand for security. But my security is your insecurity." The assertion retains its validity despite the disintegration of the USSR.

In our times, as a result of the development and pressure of the means of communication, international law has extended its influence and capacity to bring pressure—at least psychological pressure which impacts politically—on the way states and even their leaders operate. The more active role of the United Nations and especially Security Council resolutions show signs of a likely strengthening of the effectiveness of law in relations. For now, however, the type of imposed rationality, which grounds this effectiveness, does not permit us to think that we are faced with a substantial change in the conception and design of these relations. Nor is it enough for many desperate persons to cease to strive to survive at any price or to enlist somewhat unreflectively in projects whose only end is risk and violence. Suspicion and lack of confidence are still the measure of international relations.

When based on this horizon of meaning, the finitude-infinitude tension takes root as negativity within that unstable equilibrium between nations, fear of the loss and of the temporal nature of liberty of possessing. Just as the effort of muscles to hold a fist completely closed eventually requires an instant of realization, power established in the framework of a symbolic universe of domination and possession is vulnerable at some point. Security soon evaporates, and the illusion of equilibrium in imposed rationality finally fractures, in confrontation with the repressed spaces of identity and the temporarily aborted structural longing for infinity of men and peoples.

In these conditions the future becomes dark and the human situation dramatic. Certainly, the encouraging changes at the end of the cold war or the reduction and relative transparency in the possession of nuclear weapons might lead someone to reject this dramatic vision. But the question has not disappeared. On the contrary, fears have increased. Although we have delayed the possibility of a nuclear winter, we draw continually nearer to a lucid awareness of the implications of irrational economic growth in the general climatic change and the greenhouse effect. However, men and world powers are reluctant to lose their space of power and deny the character of limit situations in these threatening interrogatives. Then there are unforeseeable factors like terrorism. It appears that access to nuclear devices may be obtained by groups outside the law, which lack the capacity to foresee the consequences of their action.

The world adds to its psychosocial economic and political sufferings the ontological and existential alternative of the possibility of the death of the human species through the influence of the uncontrolled freedom of a few or for unknown, unforeseeable events, products of a hunger for security. The fleeting forms of dissuasion and self-control in the case of nuclear arsenals or the rational attempts responsibly to take charge of progress with a view to greater ecological awareness have permitted until now—in Jean Guitton's apt phrase[30]—"the benefit of avoiding dramas by replacing them with psychodramas." But "the real possibility of falling from psychodrama into drama," or worse yet into planetary tragedy, has not thereby ceased to be more present than in any other historical moment, because of the characteristic way in which power of domination is consummated.

5. Power, Liberty, and Meaning

In an aside on "the question of power" in his *History and Truth*,[31] Paul Ricoeur concludes: "the central problem of politics is *freedom*: whether the State *founds* freedom by means of its rationality, or whether freedom limits the passions of power through its resistance." Earlier,[32] considering historical events and economic and social revolutions, he noted that power so to speak has no history, that the history of power repeats itself. "The thing is that there is no real political surprise. Techniques change, human relationships depending upon things, and yet power unveils the same paradox, that of a twofold progress in rationality and in possibilities for perversion."

As in the case of Hartmann above, Ricoeur's reflections characterize what the power of domination is from our viewpoint. Although his philosophical thought is inspired by other sources, his vision of power is not different *here* from the treatment that we have seen in Foucault and de Jouvenel. The key to these shared criteria of analysis ought to be sought first in the concept of rationality with which they work—and do not substantially question—and second, in the restricted and positive use of the notion of freedom.

Doubtless, the history of each human being has always been the history of a failure to encounter himself, the history of a vain search for the infinite in things. Against what the masters of suspicion (Marx, Nietzsche, and Freud) and their less talented followers have taught, the real illusion of humanity has been its *realism*, its blind attachment to things. The immediacy of the finite is a surer psychological project than betting on transcendence. However, history and culture offer examples of how we can shake off the empirical burden of our existence. There is nothing more real than our hope to be fully. But illusion comes when hope dissolves into waiting and freedom into option. Indeed if the constitutive act of freedom does not open a meaningful horizon of our existence, the rationality of our conduct is hardly more than a mechanism of repression of the passions. The text quoted refers to this type of freedom. It offers no articulation of meaning between freedom and power but an implicit Manicheanism. Although it seems paradoxical, this Manicheanism expresses the realistic pessimism upon which the doctrine of Western political liberalism is based, which, setting aside nuances, has been adopted as a shared spirit in the rules of common social life.

This phenomenon certainly reflects political and social relations since the onset of modernity, and obviously we would have paid attention to it if we were analyzing only from the point of view of social science; but it is not essential to man. What is natural in this phenomenon is its historical, habitual character. Man is poor in spiritual possibilities, because he has chosen to be poor. He has made himself a thing with things in the complex weave which exceeds him in meaning.

However, it cannot be said that man lacks human prototypes who have risen above the narrow straits of their finite condition by placing an authentic sense on their lives. History offers them as permanent values for humanity. But these flesh and blood examples seem far away, doubtful, and weak when it is time to resist the temptation of immediacy.

It is possible that the central problem of politics is freedom. Certainly, men need to find and harmonize their spaces of identity, even in the extreme case that they are not completely conscious of their aspiration to have a place in the world. Properly speaking, this would be the true finality of politics. However, our objective here is not to investigate the historical validity of Ricoeur's affirmation, but to show the necessity that in reality, behind the discussion of the relations between freedom and power considered specifically and empirically, there is an ontological, existential exercise of freedom which predetermines these relations. Hence our insistence on the epistemological limitation of any non-philosophical approach to the essence of power.

The struggles for power, crushing freedom, violence in any form, the pettiness which humans show, are some of the manifestations of the way in which we have objectified our freedom in history. But the fact that these phenomena constitute a reality in our lives does not grant them the totality of possible meanings into which freedom and power can determine themselves.

We have shown the existence of a necessary connection of meaning between one and the other. The authenticity of any human project rests on the type of link which we establish between our freedom of being in the world and the consequences of this action. Thus, the use of power only leads to the ontological growth of the person when it is nourished in freedom to be. But it is important to repeat that this freedom to be is not grounded or enriched by splints and parapets which only express our fears and our incapacity to accept the metaphysical condition of being persons, and consequently our community with others.

Power and freedom, precisely as existentials, are essentially openness, positing the world as possibility of being. When men discover the bond in meaning which supports their achievements, that is, that aspiration to infinity which they originally share and which differentiates them specifically from every other living creature in the world, then the encounter increases the dimension of meaning for all.

Notes

1. Cf. H. Daniel Dei, "Conciencia de catástrofe, poder y libertad," in II Congreso Internacional de Filosofia del Derecho, Plata, May 19-23, 1987, vol. 1, 27-37; an expanded version of this paper appeared in 399-405 of *Revista de Filosofía de la Universidad de Costa Rica*, volume 27, no. 66, 1989; see 400 ff.

2. Sergio Daniel Labourdette, *El poder. Hacia una teoría sistemática* (Buenos Aires: Ed. de Belgrano, 1984), 2-22.

3. J. C. Smith, *Los supuestos de la Ciencia Política* (Buenos Aires: Abeledo-Perrot, 1990), 63 ff. See also Germán Bidart Campos, *El derecho constitucional del poder*, vol. 1 (Buenos Aires: Ediar) chapter 1, no. 3: "State or political power is above all social power. . . . If political power is directed at men, it is a relational structure by essence, that is it is directed at the community to order social life, which is the life of individuals in their particular reciprocal relations and in their relations with the state."

4. Carlos S. Nino, *Etica y Derechos Humanos* (Buenos Aires: Paidós, 1984).

5. Heinz Heimsoeth, *La Metafísica moderna* (Madrid: Revista de Occidente, 1966), 305 ff.

6. Heinz Heimsoeth, *La Metafísica moderna*, 307.

7. Heinz Heimsoeth, *La Metafísica moderna*, 307.

8. On our point of view about Kant's linking of metaphysics and freedom along with a criticism of the general textbook interpretation of this matter, applicable here

to the neo-Kantian movements and its implications in the philosophy of law, see above chapter 3, section 1, especially note 3.

9. Cf. Heimsoeth, *La Metafísica moderna*, 310.

10. Cf. Max Müller, *Crisis de la Metafísica*, trans. A. Klein (Buenos Aires: Editorial Sur, 1962), 167-168.

11. H. Daniel Dei, "Conciencia de Catástrofe, Poder y Libertad . . . ", 400.

12. Bertrand de Jouvenel, *On Power: Its History and the Nature of its Growth*, preface by D. W. Brogan, trans. J. F. Huntington (Boston: Beacon Press, 1962; Viking Press, 1948), 17.

13. De Jouvenel, *On Power*, 27.

14. Hans Kelsen, *General Theory of Law and State*, trans. Anders Wedberg (New York: Russell and Russell, 1961). See also J. Vilanova, "Exposición de la Teoría pura del Derecho," in *Revista de la Facultad de Derecho y Ciencias Sociales*, year 9, no. 40, 1954, 1103-1104.

15. Cf. de Jouvenel, *On Power*,28. See also the example and reflections of H. L. A. Hart in *The Concept of Law*, with a postscript edited by Penelope A. Bulloch and Joseph Raz (Oxford: Clarendon Press, 1994), especially, chapter 4, "Sovereign and Subject."

16. Michel Foucault, "Lecture Two, 14 January, 1976," 92-108, in *Power/ Knowledge: Selected Interviews and Other writings, 1972-1977*; trans. and ed. Colin Gordon (New York: Pantheon, 1980), 93. For a more complete development of Foucault's ideas about the evolution of systems of power, see his *Discipline and Punish: The Birth of the Prison,* trans. Alan Sheridan (New York: Vintage Books, second edition, 1995).

17. Foucault, "Lecture Two," 95.

18. Foucault, "Lecture Two," 96.

19. Cf. Michel Foucault, "Lecture Two," 108.

20. See de Jouvenel, *On Power*, chapter 14, and H. Daniel Dei, "Conciencia de Catástrofe, Poder y Libertad," 401 ff.

21. Thomas S. Kuhn's distinction between perception and interpretation suggested this point; see *The Structure of Scientific Revolutions*, vol. 2, no. 2, International Encyclopedia of Unified Science (Chicago: University of Chicago Press, second edition, 1970), 1975,198.

22. Cf. chapter 3 of the present work, "The Value of Freedom."

23. Again see chapter 3 of the present work, "The Value of Freedom."

24. To better explain our point of view we note that our presentation implies that the concept of freedom which we are elaborating clearly differs from Heidegger's in matters as substantial as the meaning and compass of freedom for man.

25. Frederick H. Hartmann, *The Relations of Nations* (New York: Macmillan, third edition, 1967). See also H. Daniel Dei, "Poder y poder nacional," en *Revista ESG*, no. 489, July-August,1988.

26. Frederick H. Hartmann, *The Relations of Nations*, 14-15; and 15, note 7.

27. Frederick H. Hartmann, *The Relations of Nations*, 41. Similar definitions can be found in almost all social theorists. For example Raymond Aron in *Democracy and Totalitarianism*, trans. Valence Ionescu (New York: Frederick Praeger, 1969) 88: "We mean by the word power (perhaps it would be better to say strength) an individual's ability to influence the behavior of one or more of his like." Or in *Peace and War: A Theory of International Relations*, trans. Richard Howard and Annette Baker Fox, abridged by Rémy Inglis Hall (New York: Doubleday Anchor, 1973), 44: "In a general sense, power is the capacity to do, make, or destroy." Cf. Rubén H. Zorrilla in *Principios y Leyes de la Sociología* (Buenos Aires: Emecé, 1992), 213: "I will call power that capacity of coercion, legal or not, consensual or not, arbitrary or not,

physical or only psychological, to orient and or modify the conduct of others in a determined direction (which is desired by whoever exercises power)."

28. Alvaro Zamoro, "Herra: Crítica y literatura de la violencia," *Revista de Filosofía de la Universidad de Costa Rica*, vol. 25, no. 62, 1987, 170, 172. Cf. Rafael Angel Herra, *Violencia, tecnocratismo y vida cotidiana*, Editorial de la Universidad de Costa Rica, 1991.

29. Robert Wesson, *International Relations in Transition* (Englewood Cliffs, N.J.: Prentice Hall, 1990), 33. Cf. 50-51. It is easy to find other authors who make the same point.

30. "Le Philosophe et la Cité Future," lecture delivered at the French War College, June 26, 1971. Cf. our translations with commentaries in collaboration with S. D. Maeso in "Jean Guitton: La Dimensión Metafísica de la Guerra Actual," *Revista E.S.G.*, no. 479, August-October, 1986, 29-53; Jean Guitton, *El pensamiento y la guerra* (Buenos Aires: Instituo de Publicaciones Navales, 1972). 136.

31. Paul Ricoeur, *History and Truth*, trans. and intro. Charles A. Kelbley (Evanston, Ill.: Northwestern University Press, 1965), 270. The meaning Ricoeur gives to freedom here serves to illustrate power of domination; it is helpful to contrast that with other texts where his thought would be reflected better. In this regard, his reflections in the lecture "El filósofo y el político ante la libertad," (Buenos Aires: Editorial Docencia, 1986) seem particularly helpful. In the lecture, he develops rigorously and profoundly the relation between the philosophical and political meaning of freedom. On this point he remarks at the beginning of his lecture: "The topic of my lecture sprang from a rejection: the rejection of a distribution of roles which would allot to students of politics a monopoly on the discussion about political, personal, economic, and social freedoms, and which would leave for philosophers the concern for its metaphysical meaning. . . . This disjunction between freedom according to political science and freedom according to philosophy . . . robs the philosophical notion of freedom of the particular dimension without which it gravitates toward abstraction and lie, and robs the political theorist's object of the dimension of meaning, without which his science is diminished into empiricism devoid of principle. . . . I wish to advocate a kind of philosophy for which political reflection does not constitute an optional sideline, but a level of privileged discourse; better, a point through which we must pass." We believe that our present reflections move in this direction, or so we intend.

32. Paul Ricoeur, *History and Truth*, 248.

Chapter 7

Diagnosis of the Present

1. Concerning Sophistic Values

The renowned classical scholar Werner Jaeger remarks: "In the history of the human mind, the sophists are a phenomenon quite as necessary as Socrates or Plato; in fact, without them, Socrates and Plato could never have existed."[1]

Modern scholarship supports this affirmation. Many specialists have partly rectified Plato's opinion about his contemporaries. A. Gómez Robledo cautiously defends this revision: "It still cannot be claimed that we have reached a final and conclusive judgment. As always occurs, some have gone to the opposite extreme, from denunciation to panegyric. Nevertheless, we believe that today we have enough information to make an impartial judgment about the sophists in general and about each of the sophists in particular."[2] We must acknowledge Gorgias, Hippias, Prodicus, and especially Protagoras as the protagonists of the first great effort of philosophical thought. Plato himself gives a final homage to Protagoras, the most eminent of the sophists.[3]

The sophist intellectual movement was a necessary turning point in fifth-century Greek sociopolitical and cultural development. It helped discover realities which otherwise would have remained hidden and satisfied specific educational needs of the citizenry. However, the sophist movement retained much of the moral skepticism of its origin. On the one hand, we share recent scholarly reevaluation of the movement's general historical value as well as that of some of the masters who gave it universal shape and direction. On the other hand, we feel that the terms "sophistic" and "sophist" (from which "sophism" has derived its sense as an incorrect reasoning, indeed consciously invalid reasoning)[4] do allude to a certain historical constant. It is unfair to dismiss this kind of knowledge as false in general, but sophistic at least has a utilitarian, practical sense, subject to convenience, with negative implications for its consistency as knowledge. Jaeger and other specialists point to the popularity and social power the sophists achieved, and particularly how they satisfied strictly practical social needs rather than those of theoretical and scientific order, unlike their philosophical predecessors.[5]

Hence we insist here on the distinction that Plato has Socrates make at the end of *Republic* Book V[6] between *philo-doxers* and *philo-sophers*, lovers of opinion and lovers of truth. Accordingly, when we refer to the sophists and employ the name to designate a characteristic of information and culture (not necessarily communication) in our own world, we will have in mind this kind of *doxographic* knowledge, opinion, which shines more by appearance, formal eloquence, and commonplaces, the impact of *ad hominem* or *ad populum* arguments. The type has little to do with truth, although it continuously claims to give the truth. What is worrisome about this model, or rather fashion, intellectual atmosphere, epochal paradigm, or spiritual current, according to the circles where it is practiced and the audiences it gathers, are the following: (1) it is normally accompanied by absolute ignorance of its relative, partial, interested nature; (2) if there is awareness that it is relative knowledge, it shows indifference to its moral consequences; and (3) by contrast, truth (factual, legal, or scientific) frequently lacks the social success achieved by showmanship, nor does it take possession of a space onstage where it might be applauded.

With varying nuances and awareness that go from theoreticians of postmodernism to public relations experts, we see victims and victimizers of this model of rebellion. Transformed into a model it crystallizes as a kind of power of domination which annuls the innovative capacity of existence. The ever-present idea of *commercialization* envelops us. This idea of commercialization not only has a facet of better service and of competition as the legitimate demand of what the Greeks would call *areté* (virtue, excellence). Really, commercialism feeds on consumerism, which is a way of having as mode of existence. The mark of our epoch, its style, is lack of explicit awareness of the measure and ethical limits of the instrument. The culture of commercialization (i.e., sale of image is only an aspect *in fieri*) also brings manipulation of the other and of oneself in favor of an object. Competition without clear existential horizon, without awareness of principles nor processes, means alienation, lack of lucidity, and loss of authentic sense of existence, whether we speak of one person or of the possibilities of some community.

In this section we do not attempt a moral or ideological debate about the values which control our daily life and the formal and informal rules which positively, institutionally objectify the spiritual state of our time more than its social dynamic. The social dynamic expresses interaction of different spaces of liberty and power. By contrast, the spiritual state might well be understood as the feeling of transcendence which accompanies the dialectic between the finite and the infinite in which we see ourselves involved as humans from birth to death.

The "diagnosis of the present" intends to situate us at the turning point, on the threshold between the facts of the life which shape existential possibilities into desires, affections, and thoughts, and what we visualize as the sense, the meaningful direction of this human effort. In other words, it will pay attention to futuribles,[7] certain facts which bear on the future. These permit us to take a prospective glance. Of course, we will be able to say nothing without taking a position, something unavoidable if we are alive and engaged with the sorrows of our period.

a. Law, Society, and Justice: Reflection on Thrasymachus

According to Proposition 4 of our thesis, law is regulation of power and freedom in a determined society according to the spirit of justice. The affirmation is obvious in the abstract. Nobody in his right mind objects to the necessity of rules which clearly describe modes of interaction, that is, human activities and conduct in society. Otherwise, no life in common would be imaginable. A normative order is consubstantial with the idea of society, indeed, to the idea of man, unless we are talking about a purely ahistorical biological abstraction. Let us remember in all the evidence that "man is at the very root of juridical ontology, since law is created by him and for him. Without man law is not necessary. Therefore he is at the base of ontological theorization. He creates juridical structures and modifies them; he institutes authorities and elects the value contents of the system."[8] Yet this evidence ceases to be so clear and distinct within the asphyxiating limits of schools or in the partial approaches of legal science, because differences of perspective appear as soon as we try to undertake the examination of a particular social order. It is not our intent to embrace one of those differences; there is already too much ideological opinion, pseudo-academic and genuinely academic, on this point. By contrast, a return to the ideas of power and liberty is relevant to ground our thesis and clarify what we mean by the spirit of justice in relation to these ideas. Our contribution might be the revaluation of what we deem to be the bases or, if one prefers, principles and primordial elements (not sources) of law and of the sense of justice in terms of specific anthropological contents.

In the light of this investigation, if we say that law regulates power and freedom within society, we suppose that:

1. Man *belongs* to a world and is essentially world, but he meaningfully appropriates it when he constitutes it from his space of identity, unfolding his freedom and achieving it by his power. This "space of identity" is not primarily a *topos*, a place, or a *quantum* which is bounded at a given moment. It only takes on this acceptation when it is used in military or commercial strategy or social mobility. To use an image: it is an interior journey, a path of growth in lucidity, as we defined it in section three of chapter 6.

2. Thus each man increases or restricts his space of freedom in relation to his greater or lesser ontological freedom in regard to the meaning of this world and his power to achieve it.

3. However rudimentary law is, its specific task is to assure the correspondence of presences in a society, the interaction between spaces of identity.

4. It follows that some fundamental factor must grant specific intent to this regulation or normative ordering: conformity with a "spirit of justice," *aequo animo*. Here the value of "justice" is constituted in the qualitative determination which guarantees the goal of any law. As the Stoic maxim proclaims, *ubi non est iustitia, ibi non potest esse ius*, where there is no justice, there can be no right law.

Referring to Radbruch, Battifol[9] affirms that the idea of justice implies the demand for respect toward the person in his relations with other persons. Radbruch thinks that this gives justice the character of an absolute claim and makes it the ultimate goal of law. For his part, Ross[10] accepts that the idea of justice has a role in the formation of primitive law, if it is understood as a requirement of rationality or regularity, for example, that juridical norms are formulated with the help of objective criteria. With these and other reservations he allows it to be labeled "constitutive" of the concept of law.

Nevertheless, any other support for our thesis pales compared to the hermeneutic wealth of the passage in the *Protagoras*. There Plato makes Protagoras recount the myth of Prometheus and Epimetheus, by which we can broaden the understanding of the spirit of justice in relation to the basic goal of law. Protagoras relates[11] that when Zeus ordered that the world be inhabited by men and beasts, he ordered Prometheus and his brother Epimetheus to distribute all the qualities that each species needed. Prometheus had the weakness to agree to Epimetheus's request that he be allowed to distribute gifts. He handed out all of the talents to animals. When man's time came, Epimetheus realized he had used up the available benefits. At this point Prometheus showed up to inspect his brother's performance and discovered that while the other creatures were suitably equipped, man was naked, helpless, without the ability to survive. At this juncture Prometheus decides to rob fire from Hephaestos's forge for men. With fire men were able to obtain the resources necessary for life. The only thing they could not do was to organize and live in cities. For that, *bion sophia*, the wisdom useful for life that came from having fire, was not enough. *Politiké sophia*, political wisdom, was also necessary. Because of this men lived in permanent war. When Zeus saw that the human species might become extinct, he intervened and sent Hermes to bring men respect (*aidós*) and justice (*dike*). When Hermes asked whether he should hand out the new gifts to all men alike or only to some as occurs with technical abilities, Zeus answered, to all alike, since cities could not subsist if only a minority were to be motivated by such feelings.

Two terms, *aidós* and *dikè* are important in the text we have paraphrased. We follow A. Gómez Robledo's more literal rendering,[12] in the Kantian sense of respect (*Achtung*) for moral law and justice, not as act but as *feeling*. Other scholars like Robin translate these terms as "moral consciousness" and "consciousness of law" respectively. Without rejecting these translations, we prefer to adopt Gómez Robledo's position supported by Nestle's version, because we are talking about something prior to the perception of a particular norm. Indeed, without the spirit of justice, without this disposition, law is merely an instrument of power, not just in the sense noted by Foucault, but in the most ordinary understanding of the alternative between the state's being ordered by justice or ordered by coercion, force. However, epistemologically self-limiting approaches like that of Alf Ross scorn as metaphysical these approximations to an easily verified human reality. Yet, the allegory which presents the underlying question still clarifies the discussion of justice in relation to law.

In this light we turn to Plato's Thrasymachus, not so much for his historical interest, but for the crude simplification in his discussion of justice, which lets us uncover the basic argument of a way of thinking that still exists. As everyone knows, Thrasymachus affirms that the just is only the interest of the strongest, and that in every city or state, the just is always the same, that is, the benefit of the established government.[13] Jaeger regards Thrasymachus as a representative of power philosophy. Some go further and claim that we have here the first expression of legal and political positivism. Without discussing its merits or the lack thereof, this doctrine of the law of the strongest was usual in the mentality of the period, even in the official doctrine of Athens at the moment of its crudest imperialism, as Thucydides reports in *The Peloponnesian War*.[14] Nor has the argument lost its attractiveness, even when it has been wrapped in less instinctive and more subtle terms, which are more acceptable to a well-grounded rationality. We hold that this way of conceiving law and therefore human social relations responds to an anthropological conception in which human freedom is limited to being the psychological possibility of doing, having, or possessing; hence that ethical relativism is an inevitable axiological option, and even a theoretically coherent one.

Thrasymachus's way of thinking can only produce relations of domination-submission and of human interaction marked by circumstantial suitability. Power of domination is the common denominator which animates these relations and which today shapes the horizon of meaning of human aspirations in everyday life, in science, and politics by increasingly subtle mechanisms.

b. The Paradox of Information and Power

Nowadays, the motivation of the relation information-power is expressed by the oft-heard phrase: "Information is power." We move in a sophistic atmosphere. Marshall McLuhan conveys its deterministic bent by calling it an *environment*. In this environment, that maxim forces itself on us, admits no argument. The intrusiveness of this atmosphere would have been unimaginable earlier. Within it, the freedom of possessing and the power of domination find maximum opportunity for development and for resultant forms of control and alienation. To link these terms in one proposition presents a challenge which modern, progressive man cannot elude. Urged on by consumerism, he loses his critical spirit about action. But this identification between information and power is false, because the objective of the possession of information is here power. Power is sought for the sake of power, since this stage of consciousness operates independently of the goals to which the subject believes he aspires. Consequently, there comes to be no interest in information as a source of truth. The truth is only what serves the design of increasing power, even narcissistically misinforming. This transformation inspires the general illusion that our spaces of identity are won by the material appropriation of the world.

We do not deny that opportune and confirmed information facilitates the organization of resources to develop our capabilities and improve our quality of life. But one must grant that if information is subordinated in its finality, it ends by annulling man's ability to discern. This can be observed easily not only in the use of information by the media, which play with ambiguity in the name of information, but also in the deformation that it suffers in corporations, social organizations, and state organisms.

The acritical reception of this relation is a product, we insist, of one way of exercising liberty, consciously and unconsciously. It exaggerates the utopia of modernity because we no longer need the rudimentary forms of possession and conquest, which in general are blatantly unattractive. Technology now lets us weave the matrix of an order controlled by knowledge so that domination is almost intangible, and individual consciousness lacks the capacity to discern it.

The disgraced consciousness is the paradoxical end of the relation information-power as the reality which the mode of existence founded on the freedom of possession confronts. Information reveals facts, but also produces them. The result is the uncertainty which swamps every space of power that has been won, since the nature and use of information contain the probability of securing power as well as of discovering the weakness that sustains it.

We wish to point out another trait. No one would deliberately confuse information and communication. Despite this it is hoped that better information increases our capacity to communicate. But if anything characterizes our epoch, it is precisely the lack of bonds of personal communication. Communication and information spring from distinct vital necessities. One serves efficiency, the other summons us to the arrangement of an existence which opens itself to another existence. So information operates in function of having, while communication is the space of identity which human beings can share when the freedom of being animates them. This modality of existence promotes a power which recognizes itself to be finite, wounded by *the need for the other* to achieve plenitude. In this case of communication, power unites what is divided, annuls distances, and beckons to man from a horizon with new possibilities of meaning.

c. Truth and Power

"When one talks so much about power, it is because it can no longer be found anywhere," affirms Jean Baudrillard,[15] about Foucault's obsession with forms of domination. Though the affirmation makes sense within the context of Baudrillard's theory, it misses something important. Foucault perceives that we can encounter other answers about man in the question of power. This intuition takes the form of innumerable working hypotheses throughout his work. It does not grow into a new knowledge, as he pretends and his many apologists would wish. Foucault continues to be a prisoner of the dominant paradigm of rationality which invalidates any discursive game outside of the oppositions recognized in the rules of the game. Transgression is one of these oppositions. Marxism, structuralism, neo-anarchism, or nihilist literary models like those Nietzsche proposes are natural, necessary complements which characterize the instrumental paradigm of reason, or if one prefers, what characterizes the type of production of knowledge and of the social imaginary since the beginning of western European modernity. Therefore, Foucault is willing to speak of power—*always* social power—in every way except *from its ground*. That is taboo. He is not interested in what power is, not even how it is manifested, but only in the means by which it is exercised[16] to determine man's life. He admits history, criticism, sociology, but not philosophy. In the precise sense we use here, a metaphysical approach to the phenomenon of power is a radical investigation which brings us to question the legitimacy of the instrument with which we are working rather than its consequences. Without that there is no conceptual break, hardly more than a turn of the screw, or a new light upon the results. Consequently, it is difficult to unearth the why of the *ubiquitous* character of power correctly observed by Foucault.[17] But we discover that power is an existential, when we situate ourselves on the metaphysical level of analysis. If so, we must always deal with it. Its ubiquitous character is no surprise. Rather, the fact reveals and validates its meaning from our perspective.

Strictly speaking there is no new history of power. Nor can we properly speak of a new history of truth. It would seem that every step of Foucault's work retains an assumption imposed by its revolutionary origin. Certainly, "truth itself has a history,"[18] but to what truth are we referring? We might refer to a "kind of internal history of truth, the history of a truth that rectifies itself in terms of its own principle of regulation . . . as it is constructed in or on the basis of a history of the sciences," or of what he denominates an "external, exterior history of truth" formed "where a certain number of games are defined—games through which one sees certain forms of subjectivity, certain object domains, certain types of knowledge come into being." In either case we speak of *the* truth as men have imagined it from the mode of existence of *having*.[19]

The truth thus construed might more exactly be called *ideology*, that is a knowledge of total integration, where philosophical *questions* are transformed into problems of casuistry so that their capacity to constitute new searches is annulled. Therefore, the scientific paradigms and philosophical systems of legitimation (like Thomism, positivism, or Marxism) have functioned historically as instruments of social power, as soon as they came to be incorporated into the immune system of the dominant rationality.

The search for the truth is one of the ways in which power, as an objectification of man's freedoms, configures a space of identity. But the *possession* of the truth or the desire to convert it into property is already the expression of the fear of freedom to be, in awareness of one's finitude. In these circumstances, the search for the truth is displaced by interest, centered in the justification, or lack thereof, of the legitimacy of the spaces of power which social subjects occupy and in the *efficacy* of those spaces. Whereas the search for the truth sets man out on a path of growing lucidity by the open nature of the search, interest for the truth shields man in knowledge-consumerism, spurred on by the need for psychological security provided by the fantasy of rest in what has been structured; the attitude derived from this mode of existence is *installation* as a form of life.

For purposes of our investigation we want to emphasize:

1. What the truth is, is a metaphysical question. Consequently, to affirm that it is absolute or relative is of itself a proposition whose validity is meaningful only in the framework of ideological disputes and reveals, with less subtlety in one case and greater ambiguity in the other, a kind of dogmatic thought.

2. By contrast, what truth is in a determined situation is an epistemological problem. Therefore, inquiry in this area strives to point out and apply conceptual instruments and suitable materials to ponder it. Since the problem of meaning derived from this task is occupied with determining whether a proposition is true or false, it has no relation to the ontological, existential question of the meaning (sense) of the *truth*.

3. A frequent error that also provokes either irresponsible acceptance or blind opposition is the affirmation that truth is relative. This is simply to confuse different modes of apprehending truth with the nature of truth itself. So we say that the question of truth (what it is and if it exists) is a metaphysical, not a logical or epistemological, question.[20] To reduce the debate to these terms is a hazard to which the relations of power and domination condemn us.

4. In the search for meaning which mobilizes the person who has placed himself in the disposition of freedom and power to be, truth acts as the possibility of new meaningful horizons for his existence. It makes his finitude clear to him at the same time as it nourishes his vocation to transcendence in a search which acquires its meaning in the option for the risk of being free. In a position of serenity (not rest) on this path, man is not preoccupied by any positive answer. He knows, experiences, to speak expressively, lives the existence of truth in ontological consistency, which, being liberated from the weight of the nature of things, returns to him.

d. Language Games

In this section we wish to work on the catchphrase "language game" in relation to the results of discourse and to prepare the way to ask whether indeed post-modernity represents the abandonment of the great legitimating discourses. How does this *philosophical* proposition come to prove what is known as the "nature of the social bond" in postmodern society, beyond the unilateral treatment of analytic philosophy within which the expression was born?[21] The topic is important not only because it will permit us further on to accompany Jean-François Lyotard[22] critically in accentuating the pragmatic side of language with Wittgenstein, but also we will have occasion to return once more to the problems of information, communication, and power. In this regard, we would like to call upon the optimistic affirmations of Gianni Vattimo[23] regarding the advent of the society of communication and the link that we believe can be established with Wittgenstein's notion of the plurality of linguistic usages.

Let us begin at the beginning. What are language games? If we wish to be faithful to the spirit of Wittgenstein,[24] we must explain the term by showing examples of its use and describing situations into which these examples fit and work, instead of appealing to a definition that could not exhaust it or would contain it confusedly. Indeed, this central notion ought to make clear that "to speak of language is part of an activity or form of life," as our author says before enumerating examples. So, the fundamental thing about language is not meaning but use, understanding how it works. Therefore, it can be compared to a game. This conception implies the abandonment of the basic theses of the *Tractatus Logico-Philosophicus* having to do with the logical structure of facts, the denotative interpretation of meaning, and the essential presupposition of logical atomism (that it is possible to reduce the complex to the absolutely simple). Now, the essence of language does not lie in its descriptive function, and its structures do not correspond to the structures of reality. Thus, the elevation of science's declarative or descriptive language to paradigm status is rejected. Rather, there exists a plurality of uses of languages which can be imagined as language games. Just as context, that is, the language game, determines what must be considered simple or complex,[25] so also use, pragmatic language, produces meaning. If this is so, avenues open up to permit an understanding of this thinker free from the limits of the neopositivist school, among which, strange as it may seem, was assumed a real metaphysical point of departure that we have previously described.

Far from being disseminated in mere discourse, meaning is paradoxically multiplied in new senses. In a development perhaps unexpected by Wittgenstein himself, the ontological vacuum that every text expresses, even the text of man's own daily life in postmodern circumstances, might account for his finite dimension. Thus philosophy would return to its source: "place its feet on the hard ground" of existence without a game of subterfuge. Because, "if semantic dissemination hides any symbolism, possibly it is that of contemporary individualism or erratic personalism in the confusion of the social mass."[26] In classical terms, this involves a state of the soul, which will surely search for a new ontological, existential horizon of meaning, because human life is not an artificial game. Derrida's "game of meaningful references"[27] is a good intellectual entertainment for literature and disenchanted intellectuals, but life is not fiction. Even pretenses are constructed as an inauthentic response to the challenge of being free. The task is to meet this challenge entirely, pass through the state of "training" (spiritual adolescence), or else to passively accept the meanings which emerge from the game.

However, for now let us renew our investigation. Dominique Lecourt's penetrating critical analysis of logical positivism, *El orden y los juegos*, makes a telling observation that recalls some of Foucault's analyses and their counterparts in Barthes and Eco about the function of literature and the power of language:[28]

> The concept of language games, certainly has a radical character. Wittgenstein wants to make us understand that language is a practice to which we are submitted, affiliated but not masters. Taken seriously, his thesis says that when we engage in the practice of language, there is not an already constituted 'we' that takes part, but rather we are constituted as such by the practice. The most enigmatic of his texts try to make us understand that there is never the preexistence of a 'subject'—and 'I'—in language. . . . Let us say furthermore," Lecourt adds, "the strongest consequence of the 'social' aspect of the 'language game' and its remission to 'life forms,' is that the constitution of the 'subject' of language (and therefore of knowledge) supposes not only language, but rather in language, what some propose to call the dimension of 'discourse.'[29]

We will not direct the commentary to questions that we cannot clarify here. We only wish to note that the theme carries us toward the discussion of the "nature of the social bond." However, we would wish to ask whether this new vision of the phenomenon of language can facilitate the transparency of human communication by way of the value placed on existential, personal, and communal ties, or whether we simply are again in the presence of a refined scheme of the legitimation of relations of domination-submission, as long as we do not know which players are imposing the rules.

This interrogative brings us back to Lyotard, who makes three observations about language games: "The first is that their rules do not carry within themselves their own legitimation, but are the object of a contract, *explicit or not*, between players (which is not to say that the players invent the rules)." The emphasis in the passage quoted is ours. We think that if the rules were not explicit there would not be transparency in the game and, therefore, language would only produce alienating or simulated effects of discourse. The criticism of legitimation produced by the so-called traditional discourse of philosophy would seem to move on this ground. Some players, however, have not stopped dictating rules. But we still do not see that the need for legitimation has disappeared, even if we take Lyotard's approach. "The second is that if there are no rules, there is no game, that even an infinitesimal modification of one rule alters the nature of the game, that a 'move' or utterance that does not satisfy the rules does not belong to the game they define. The third remark is suggested by what has just been said: every utterance should be thought of as a 'move' in a game."[30] From these observations Lyotard extracts two principles which control his method of analysis to explain the characteristics of the social bond in postmodern society: (1) "to speak is to fight, in the sense of playing, and speech acts fall within the domain of a general agonistics. This does not necessarily mean that one plays in order to win. A move can be made for the pleasure of its invention. . . . But, undoubtedly, even this pleasure depends on a feeling of success won at the expense of an adversary." In great measure the difficulties inherent in Wittgenstein's notion of language game have been brought out by different authors, among them, the concept of general struggle that Lyotard derives in his essay. (2) As a complement to the first principle, the author enunciates the next major proposition: "the observable social bond is composed of language 'moves.'"[31]

At the peak of this examination we end with more new interrogatives rather than threads leading to greater conceptual clarity about the problem—we do not ask for solutions. Certainly, each of the statements quoted goes toward corroborating one or another of our theses insofar as it only understands social bonds on the basis of instrumental power, domination. If we agree that the meaning of language is found in social practice which produces language games, that is, in their use, it is clear that the general struggle to which Lyotard referred tries to win spaces of power (in the sense of having), more than to make communication transparent, that is, to open existence to lucidity as a form of life. What is left, then, are abstractions (make-believe) or the game of discourse without referent. There are only texts which generate texts. There is no connection with man's life and concrete existence. This is the contrary of what Wittgenstein seemed to have in mind. The pure pragmatic of language is a mere fiction. It would only produce vacuums of existential meaning, because it only legitimates and takes as its paradigm the discourse of power emanating from domination. However, this discourse is not constructed without the decisions and desires of men. Or else, if we leave behind Thrasymachus's style, there are no more players who impose the rules. Have we not suggested that our contemporaries have left the adolescences of the discourses of power still subject to the moral disease which demanded a justification that was valid for itself and for society, only to give way to an analytic version of the Nietzchean superman's "everything goes" for the deciders of those games? Is this the "to continue to dream, knowing that one dreams" of Nietzsche in *The Gay Science*, the nihilist aggiornamento of the old sophistic methods which inspires contemporary western beliefs?

For a moment, let us aspire to Gianni Vattimo's optimism. According to the Italian philosopher, far from Calderón de la Barca's "life is dream," Nietzsche's phrase seems to concentrate the essence of superman in the world of intensified communication. We admit not completely understanding what Vattimo means by this, above all if "to go on dreaming" is interpreted as the task assigned to future humanity.[32] What seems clear is that we humans are at our own mercy, once modernity's idea of a central historical rationality is smashed.

The end of history or whatever we want to call the phenomenon,[33] to our mind, is rather the sign of a will to power which has shaken off the moral necessity of legitimating its ambitions of power, of domination, even by "metaphysical" discourse. The end of history is really the end of *a* history which has entered into crisis. On its sickbed it develops a new universal discourse without abandoning the spirit of Thrasymachus; the democratic strategy of including cultural minorities enables it to abort their capacity to unfold their own emancipatory spirit. The independence of contemporary man is only dependence on language games which involve him without his being able to really participate in the moves, without giving them new meanings. We ought, therefore, to correct our previous affirmation: more than remaining at the mercy of ourselves, we are products of the context of the game of supply and demand. Postmodernity is precisely the culture in which that rationality now operates as informative persuasion, a hash of exchanges of opinions where the truth is shaded to optimize consumption. In this terrain it is difficult to grow in personal commitment which communication implies, at least communication in its most precise and human sense. "We are more in a world of expressions, perhaps of shouts, than of communication."[34]

However, Vattimo's thesis proclaims: "Along with the end of imperialism and colonialism, another decisive factor in both the dissolution of the idea of history and the end of modernity is the advent of the society of communication."[35] Indeed it is necessary to know whether postmodern society is becoming an effectively "transparent" society. He adds, "What I am proposing is: (a) that the mass media play a decisive role in the birth of a postmodern society; (b) that they do not make the postmodern society a more 'transparent' but more complex, even chaotic society; and finally (c) that it is precisely in this relative 'chaos' that our hopes of emancipation lie." The doubt is about the subject of hope: is it humanity or European society? Ethnocentrism is an evil that we all endure and we cannot see that it is uprooted from the text that Vattimo proposes, although we value his notable effort to comprehend and include other visions of the world.

These *Weltanschauungen* are presented by the mass media as fragments of a human universe *out there,* in full view. Yet they are not seen as containing the ontological drama of an existence which aspires to the freedom to be itself. In Vattimo, as with the European thinkers whose lucidity is undeniable, the question is still contaminated with ethnocentrism. We understand that this is suggested in the book we are quoting at the end of the chapter whose title is an interrogative: "Postmodern—a transparent society?" "In the society of generalized communication and the plurality of cultures, the encounter with other cultures and forms of life is perhaps less in the imagination than it was for Dilthey. 'Other' possibilities of existence are realized before our very eyes, in the multiplicity of 'dialects,' and in the different cultural universes opened up by anthropology and ethnology. . . . To live in a pluralistic world means to experience freedom as a continual oscillation between belonging and disorientation." A sincere sentiment, but inadmissible for other Europeans who have not yet noticed the vulnerability of an identity, which finds itself the orphan of a grounding reason, and which seeks in a new legitimating discourse its possibility of being. In the last analysis, the problem of the crisis of European rationality is a problem of uprootedness, because an instrument of domination which reclaims its privileges has decentered the unity of awareness of the world. Here again, freedom of being and freedom of having show their differences, for we find nostalgia for a lost security (the conception of unity for history) and commotion about the daily irruption of the other, the strange, primitive (ethnic, sexual, religious, cultural minorities), which has incorporated itself to life as an object of consumption. Freedom as continual oscillation between belonging and alienation is a tragic form of the risky freedom of having, which threatens, for now, the bases for sustaining the spaces of power of dominion it has achieved. Vattimo goes on: "Such freedom is problematic. As an effect of the media it cannot be guaranteed and remains a possibility still to be recognized and taken up (the media can always and everywhere be the voice of 'Big Brother,' or of stereotypical banality, void of meaning . . .). Moreover, we ourselves still do not have a clear idea of its physiognomy and so have difficulty in seeing oscillation of freedom. Individually and collectively, we still have a deep-seated nostalgia for the reassuring, yet menacing closure of horizons. Nihilistic philosophers like Nietzsche and Heidegger (but also pragmatists like Dewey and Wittgenstein) in demonstrating that being does not necessarily coincide with what is stable, fixed and permanent, but has instead to do with events, consensus, dialogue, and interpretation, try to show us how to take the experience of the oscillation of the postmodern world as an opportunity for a new way of being (finally, perhaps) human."

As we will see below, it is possible that the dystopia of postmodernity is the critical transition to a more lucid awareness of humanity, but it is also indubitable that for now its discourse directs it to propagate a cynical rationality in the oldest and most exact sense of the term, which permits us to operate without the inefficiency of moral conscience. Vattimo's optimism has merit, as do his reflective efforts to order the chaos of signs which the reality of the world begets daily. We only note that in games certain players cheat and, in this matter, philosophy can do something more than clarify problems of language.

2. Postmodern Culture

"Against the deep structures and their truth, appearances and their destiny? Be that as it may, we are living today in non-sense, and if simulation is its disenchanted form, seduction is its enchanted form.

"Anatomy is not destiny, nor is politics: seduction is destiny. It is what remains of a magical, fateful world, a risky, vertiginous and predestined world; it is what is quietly effective in a visibly efficient and stolid world.

"The world is naked, the king is naked, and things are clear. All of production, and truth itself, are directed toward disclosure, the unbearable 'truth' of sex being but the most recent consequence. Luckily, at bottom, there is nothing to it. And seduction still holds, in the face of truth, a most sibylline response, which is that 'perhaps we wish to uncover the truth because it is so difficult to imagine it naked.'"

Thus ends Jean Baudrillard's book *Seduction*.[36] The splendid text bares the *pathos* (to continue with the metaphor) of postmodernity.[37] We do not experience the loneliness of radical finitude as in existentialism nor do we find the new philosophical skepticism's cautious abstention that warns about western man's *hybris*. Much less do we have the consequences of the contentiousness that mobilized the countercultural movement. Rather, this precise critical reflection tidies up the obscure side of nihilism's omnipotence and its hedonist presupposition. There is no vacuum of meaning because there is no meaning. Freedom has chosen its own death: the impossibility of meaning. There is neither expectation nor hope,[38] but indifference, burlesque, with the disposition of mind that accompanies a state of crisis. If postmodernity were the acceptance of a crisis, the result would not be superficiality. But the pathos of postmodern culture is not tragic. It does not desire some transformation. It is the expression of unease which attempts to find itself in the emptiness of pure contingency. Accordingly we find sham, exaltation of momentary pleasure, enjoyment of artificial imagination, recreational use of sex, autism of the deconstruction of the text, the plurality of little discourses without recipients, the deontologized heterogeneity of its manifestations, the fragmentation of an order of sense and meaning itself. Postmodern man is rootless, without the capacity of accounting for the universality of his presence in the world. The sophist's representation aspired to persuade in order to win a space of power. By contrast the postmodern is satisfied with the game of seduction. Masks suppress the real with the paradoxical *transvestite*[39] freedom, where one pretends to be what one is not. The object is to avoid the consequences of human sexual commitment, no past, no future, no history, no identity. The only possibility is in the flight from any existential scarring. Everything is permitted in this total game except to undress seduction and deprive us of its attractions, because that would be to expose us to the challenge of meaning.

Innumerable interrogatives confront us, including whether our own discourse is self-contradictory, since the phenomenon of postmodernity is presented to analysis as a packed bouquet of diverse, ambiguous, and confused expressions. Its nature is so little transparent that the current debate goes from interpreting it as a radical rupture with modernity to qualifying it as a cheap and perverted copy of modernity. Let us see. Our theme is the problem of freedom and power in postmodern society. The question is: What freedom and consequently what power gives rise to this postmodern pathos? According to what we have seen so far, the answer is quite obvious: only freedom of having and power of domination can leave man hopeless, leave him disenchanted with the world, and submerge him in indifference. Far from increasing the capacity to choose as liberalism thinks, consumerism restricts freedom in terms of option and devours its potentiality for meaning. What is revealed in the arrangement of ontological freedom is no longer personal being, but identity achieved by affinity with the worldly character of things. If pure exteriorization is the nature of the *real*, subterfuge is the answer and seduction is the Dionysiac passion for life. Will not this excess of reality—hyperreality as postmodern thinkers themselves remark—produce the fragmentation of power in the heart of society and lead finally to the ecstasy of life?

However, our doubts are not calmed. Let us accept with Lyotard that postmodern "designates the state of our culture following the transformations, which, since the end of the nineteenth century, have altered the game rules for science, literature, and the arts."[40] Then, how do we relate postmodernity with so-called postindustrialism, the material effect or cause—we will not discuss which now—of these transformations? The first answer that occurs to us finds solid arguments in the reasons above; indeed, it would permit us to again validate our thesis about the substantive connection between freedom and power and their character as existentials. But we wish to emphasize something more, about which we will occupy ourselves in the next chapter. If postmodernity is not also characterized by a syncretism of forms and contents, it would be difficult to link it to the optimist efficiency that sustains the postindustrialist mystique. In fact, nothing here is contradictory. Lyotard himself defines this state of culture for the "more developed societies," that is, for hegemonic countries. Only by defect, bastardy, submission, dependence, or whatever it may be called, does it represent the spiritual state of other societies. Postmodernity is the name we give to the crisis of a kind of society and a modality of rationality; consequently, in principle, we ought to consider the phenomenon an endogenous problem. But postmodernity also seems to initiate a new and more subtle discourse of power. In the discourse we encounter the true reason for the potency of its planetary effect. If postmodern culture seems to operate with a logical vacuum and with strategies of seduction without renouncing scientific-technological delights and consequent satisfactions, it is because it has already thrown overboard certain moral commitments that were still present in the metaphysical constructions of modernity, and which required the legitimation of noble universal values like progress, freedom, civilization, the primacy of the spirit, welfare, or even the enviable fate of the unfolding of reason. Postmodernity's ahistorical and acultural vocation—if we may consider it a vocation—perfectly suits the modality of the power of domination and, therefore, the character of science and the nature of cybernetic knowledge. It is more efficient than the metaphysical discourses which cannot elude the question of man. Subterfuge and calculation banish the phantom of the uncertainty of freedom and activate reality without confronting it, without the commitment of existence. They make the future present in representation. The pragmatics of language do not seem to be enough to keep our feet on the hard floor.

a. Dystopia: Culmination of the Project of Modernity

Lyotard relates the transformations which give rise to postmodernity to the crisis of narratives. We define narrative as a discourse or narration which places man and his activities within a totalizing, inclusive horizon. So narratives always have a legitimating character. They justify the place to which man has acceded or desires to reach. Explicitly or implicitly they interpret the history which man protagonizes. In their more systematized forms they constitute the structure of philosophies of history. In the academic history of thought we encounter completely formulated specimens of a philosophical sense of history, but the Hegelian system is the paradigm of these great narratives or metanarratives, capable of including particular events of individuals and peoples in one vision. Postmodern culture represents incredulity toward this type of narrative. In social practice and under the scrutiny of contemporary scientific knowledge, these magnificent constructions of thought have been revealed as fables.

The existential dimension of this spiritual state is such that we can affirm that postmodernity takes root in this incredulity. It is its figure, if one wishes. This incredulity is even directed to those old narratives which are acknowledged to have sired the spiritual crisis, such as speculative idealism and modernity's account of emancipation. Does the incredulity exempt postmodernity from having given birth or suffering the birth pains of a new metanarrative? Does this spiritual state not constitute a manifestation of the internal logic of these great narratives? Is it possible that irrationality, which has fed hopes of omnipotent human autonomy in hegemonic societies, has been set loose outside the control of reason? The first of these interrogatives will be answered in the next section. The other two will be considered now.

Within our investigation in conformity with Proposition 5 of the thesis we advance, we affirm that postmodernity is a dystopian manifestation of the utopia of modernity. It is thus not only a "crisis of metaphysical philosophy," as Lyotard claims,[41] although almost all authors who have discussed the topic simply echo him, whether or not they are strictly postmoderns. Just as we remarked in the question of truth, here, too, the how is confused with the what. If it were really a question of metaphysical philosophy as some authors maintain, we would not see the sense of Lyotard's asking, "where can legitimation reside after meta-narratives?" Or is there some legitimation that is not a narrative? In reality, the expression "crisis of metaphysical philosophy" should allude without anthropocentric ambiguities to *one* model of metaphysical construction, since its exhaustion does not necessarily imply that metaphysical questions as such cease to have force as such. A historical model of rationality can configure those fundamental ontological, existential responses, but it does not close them as interrogatives, nor should these interrogatives be thematized in only one perspectival direction. Rather we find the crisis of one type of metaphysical knowledge, of one type of imagined rationality which is revealed, incapable of taking over the metaphysical questions which pursue man.

Why do we say that, as the culmination of modernity's project, postmodernity is a dystopia? For two reasons: (1) There exists a continuity of meaning between the projects of modernity and the material state of postindustrial societies; and (2) there is a direct line of communication, an internal, immanent link, between the utopia and the dystopia. In modernity's utopian component, imagination rids itself of authority and of unsatisfactory order to project itself into a place that is nowhere, into an indeterminate future, which is to constitute a new state of humanity, with the confidence in one's own capacity to amplify the conditions of lucidity of man and society. Like all utopian projects, it confronts the problem of power itself and its most efficacious transformation. It offers alternatives to overcome existing conditions that postulate an amplified freedom, born in the critique of reason and historically achieved. This would be a *eutopia*, which mobilizes all man's strength and his desire for permanence and converts it sufficiently to defy the contingency of reality and reduce everything which opposes itself to it to the choice of reason thus founded. By contrast, the utopian component of postmodernity is exasperated as dystopia, a bad place, in social practices, and expresses itself as a catastrophic denunciation, the last of the forms and the dismantling of the cosmos. "The difference between utopia and dystopia is only axiological, but not material. What changes are the subject of discourse's judgments of appreciation, not the contents of the text," affirms an article[42] by the Spanish thinker Núñez Ladeveze, where textual comparison shows that narrative contents, legal or axiological descriptions of the type of narratives recognized as utopian, can be the object of absolutely opposed ethical considerations. "Utopia is a project to be realized, a hope founded in immanent principles [that is, the effort of human action to be self-sufficient in the historical realm; and its process takes place either by way of the reduction of history to the concepts of reason or by way of reduction of reason to an epiphenomenon of its material condition], in the earthly calculation of a reason which tries to blend itself into the whole, to resolve reality, to embrace the absolute socially considered. But utopia is also the dystopian inversion of the project, when the hope achieved leaves only the faded trace of an always frustrated desire."[43]

In his *Lectures on Ideology and Utopia*,[44] Paul Ricoeur repeats that utopias constitute an imaginative variation on the nature of power. In this sense he reaffirms their role as a recourse for periods like ours in which "everything is blocked by the systems which have failed but which cannot be overcome." Far from being the "end of utopias," postmodernity is the naked, dystopian face of modernity's utopia. This explains the flight into seduction, disenchantment with life, and festive enjoyment of the freedom of having. This is what makes it insolent and provocative, although complacent and counterrevolutionary. It does not aspire to open new ontological, existential horizons for man, because its horizon continues to be that of instrumental reason, as manager of the spaces under the power of domination. Therefore, it rejects or disqualifies utopian creativity and the critical function of other human subjects which do not belong to dominant societies, with the same interested deafness that accompanies colonial adventures in homage to a new idea of progress: communications on a planetary scale (better, "informatocracy") and a type of *homogeneous* knowledge which optimizes material production and well-being. Self-proclaimed heterogeneity is the aesthetic game and the ephemeral expression. As Vattimo perceives it,[45] "The most eye-catching feature of the passage from utopia to heteropia is the liberation from the ornament and the lightening of being which is its ontological significance." Vattimo expects an exit from the crisis, which we fear is the subtle containment of the role of any nondominant utopia in which the search for truth still aspires to be a protagonist.

The "world of visible efficacy," whose ideology is technocratic, is necessarily prolonged in postmodern culture and prepares a great new narrative of domination in it and from it. As the Costa Rican philosopher Rafael Angel Herra observes well, "to think is also to hide."

> Technocratism today represents the novel, coherent integration in history of the two poles of knowing a semantic, functional integration which adequately coincides with the logical, directed fusion of interest and theory. Pragmatist and positivist, technicist, and sober, efficient and lustless, antispeculative and quantified, stateless and dominating, transnational and enterprising, cyberman reduces truth to thing and thing to truth whose conditions of possibility he sets himself. This man is the state, the transnational corporation, the engineer of conduct at a distance, the thinker of technology, the genius of conduct, whether malign or unconscious. Thought presents itself in Heidegger as revealing. But is that so? Isn't there a thought which hides? . . . there are kinds of knowledge which, although they possess scientific applicability, hide themselves from themselves as ideology precisely because success in the realization of an idea hides the realm of their origin and of their ends. Technocratism is the ideology of control which hides its agent. Technocratic thought is the theoretical act of this occultation.[46]

In the light of these arguments we should perhaps emphasize that the end of the utopias announced by critics and defenders of postmodernity is really a literary figure in the gestation of a great narrative to come which prolongs and perfects the objectivizing freedom and the power of domination which inspired modernity's vocation to being, the utopia of the absolute in the immanence of the control of historical and cultural processes. The dystopian experience of the ideal of humanity seems to unburden man of metaphysics' imperfect existential shocks. In the manner of Orwell, Huxley, or perhaps closer to Skinner,[47] it assures him pretended enjoyment of programmed freedom in the general framework of civilizing development (that of the technologically developed societies). Such development is supposedly capable of articulating the deficient utopian flights of ontological freedom among "nondesigned" cultures of the less developed societies.

b. The Great Postmodern Narrative

Given how the incipient discourse of knowledge in postmodern culture sets itself up in opposition to the "vulgarity" of the narratives of traditional cultures, Lyotard's abstract, impersonal question could very well be reformulated. Instead of, "Where could legitimation reside after meta-narratives?" we would ask in existential and *realist* terms, "Where will man find a new metanarrative to sustain him?" We said above that this interrogative goes to the root of the question of the meaning of man within hegemonic societies. Lyotard's allusion to "the societies with which we are concerned"[48] betrays the petulant tranquillity of one who knows himself installed on the axis of history. He does not step out of the point of view of the one who decides. The rest of societies do not make history; they adapt themselves to the designer's model with greater or lesser docility. In good worldly terms, it is a matter of turning the goals of modernity's emancipatory and enlightened enterprise around to current times, reducing operating costs and increasing the productivity of the rationality still tinged with morality, the idea of God, or other unproductive vagaries. Contrary to what some believe, this does not require abandoning the ideas of progress and unity of history. The first is in control, dusted off, as an irresistible force of the new narrative, an unavoidable postmodern *moira*. The second has changed subjects. The protagonist is not man or a culture. Now the protagonist is supposed to be planetary expansion of the communications media (which have owners) and of complex, computerized knowledge (which has interested backers). Therefore, we affirm that postmodern man *already* lives the experience of his own narrative; it is constructed upon the replacement of the universal emancipatory ideal by the satisfaction of consumption, the replacement of the Enlightenment synthesis of knowledge by the guaranteed receipts of data banks and the development of the spirit of the mass media as the social articulation of communication. In other words, the great narrative of postmodernity revolves around the principle of the performability of the "being" of efficiency, capable of being achieved in politics, economics, education, sport, science, religion, law, procreation, indeed in life itself as personal, social, natural possibility. The freedom of having and the power of domination taken as the modes of being of our existence ground this principle. If metaphysical discourses are discourses of power, postmodernity's new discourse is no less metaphysical, because it rejects them as attempts to legitimate the being of existence. What traditional metaphysical construction, including positivism, has not begun with the criticism of the previous system? Did Nietzsche, Heidegger, Wittgenstein, or even Foucault refrain from voicing opinions about the constitution of the world or man's destiny? Sometimes academic hedonism or the bad conscience of Enlightenment intellectuals functions like bureaucrats who make their procedures mysterious to guarantee themselves a space of identity, a recognition, realizing that they are unable to earn it with an authentic commitment in life. We must presume there is no naiveté in this, for what do we call metaphysics? The scheme of the discourse, or rather the thematization of certain questions?

The spiritual state resulting from this dynamic of knowledge works on men in two different ways. For those who belong to the countries of the north in their interests, not just geographically, the future is the feeling of a current satisfaction; it is present and already being achieved. There is no sense in dreaming about the future or in dreaming at all. The utopian recourse as a prospective motor ends by being an outmoded tool, too tied to the spontaneity of freedom. The perspectives are determined by circumstantial utility, and alterations can be simulated in time to foresee their effects and summon the means of corrections. The accumulation of instants of power configures life. There is no place or legitimation grounded on the values of truth and justice, unless the maneuver of power circumstantially demands a rhetorical appeal to it. If the "only creditable goal is power,"[49] it should be repeated that this is because the dystopian revelation of the humanist or idealist project has stripped the hidden meaning from modern freedom. So naturally, as Lyotard goes on to say, "Scientists, technicians, and instruments are purchased not to find truth but to augment power." The attempt to optimize its efficacy can impel us to overcome the crisis of discourse and to assure the continuity of the project. If technical criteria have steadily more influence as criteria of truth, and the normativity of law gives way to performability of procedures, it is because confidence in human reason is discredited. The homogeneity of the system can absorb contradictions. Whoever exercises his freedom so as to make this type of power his place of identity, cannot do other than convert this technocratic alienation into a legitimation.

The only possible social order is marked by functionality and efficiency to maintain the connection of monads of identity won in the progress of commensurability and control of the alternatives of others, who play or believe they are playing the same game. Scholars agree that this society only admits two types of players: deciders and executors. The men and cultures who do not belong to the first type of countries are executors without any capacity of their own to express a sentiment about the future which would alter the rules of the game; moreover, strictly speaking, they are a potential market for consumption, "*passive* consumers" in the legitimating narratives of deciders. Thus, in this new narrative, we are only allowed to think and make one knowledge, one culture, and one existence, which is marginal in relation to the paradigm of knowledge and of the life of the deciders, and to hope partially to assimilate the world of "performative competence" where it is important that knowledge be useful and not exactly true, that it can be sold, and that it turns out efficacious in increasing power.

Existence as the product of the freedom of having is a probability conditioned in the universe of a matrix whose input and output we do not know. Or is it that we think we do not know it? The social subject is dissolved in the formability of functioning. He will be a variable/datum that can be processed in the context of a genetic program, if we can reach a consensus as Skinner firmly believes.[50] Death as the possibility of existence mediated by the alternative nothingness comes to reinforce the desire for worldly possession and to savor the pure competitive pleasure of the game of life instead of choosing tragic authenticity. We believe that freedom which is transcended in finitude cannot help but aspire to know itself infinite in the contingency of the world. We are only as much as we possess, and we are more if we possess more. To be for death is not foreign to a being for the instant. Understanding one proposition to be the other may not be a bad understanding. Thus, the description of this society, which is a part of our "life circumstance," is well conveyed in Lyotard's assertion, "The social bond is linguistic,"[51] which amounts to affirming the explosion of community.

Since the pragmatics of language have replaced efforts of semantic approximation, links of understanding are abandoned. If, as Lyotard himself suggests,[52] legitimation must come from linguistic practice and communicative interaction, it surely cannot be by dodging ontological, existential questions. What stands out as primary amid the multiplicity of language games is precisely their use. In consequence, we might well imagine that those who possess know-how in the manner of classic sophistic marketing have access to the control of society. Precisely, this is not a game for everyone, but only for those who play a role in the consolidation of power.

In these conditions, how are the norms constituted? What can we expect from law? In what state is the principle of rationality to be found which informs every juridical ordering? Can Alf Ross's idea of objective justice be more rational if the judge is an intelligent computer that an expert system operates? Is legal philosophical thought capable of revealing the assumptions that already condition future legal systems, or will it be limited to legitimating them by way of new modes of the same waning philosophizing? What will the function of law be, if the coming human universe is cybernetic monotonality and communicational interaction by modular juxtapositions?

Notes

1. Werner Jaeger, *Paideia: The Ideals of Greek Culture*, vol. 1, *Archaic Greece: The Mind of Athens*, trans. from second German ed. by Gilbert Highet (New York: Oxford University Press, second ed., 1965), 291.

2. Platón, *Los seis grandes temas de su filosofía* (Mexico City: Fondo de Cultura Económica and Universidad Nacional Autónoma de México, 1974), 470 ff. Cf. also Mario Untersteiner, *I Sofisti* (Turin: Einaudi, 1949); by the same author, *Sofisti, testimonianze e frammenti*, 5 vols. (Florence: La Nuova Italia, 1967); Adolfo Levi, *Storia della Sofistica*, (Naples:, 1986).

3. "For I believe he died about seventy years old, forty of which he spent in the practice of his art; and he retains undiminished to this day the high reputation he has enjoyed all that time" *Meno*, 91 E, in Plato, *Laches, Protagoras, Meno Euthydemus*, Loeb Library translation, W. R. M. Lamb (Cambridge, Mass.: Harvard University Press, 1924, 1962), 341.

4. See José Ferrater Mora's article in *Diccionario de Filosofía* (Buenos Aires: Editorial Sudamericana) with which we strongly agree.

5. Werner Jaeger, *Paideia*, vol. 1, 288.

6. Plato, *Republic*, Book V, 475d and ff., especially 476d.

7. *Futurible* here means "what we grasp as a sign at present but what will be manifested in the future," so that it is constituted as a fact bearing the future. The word comes from the Latin *futurabile*, plural *futurabilia*: it is usually translated as "future contingent" or "possible" and technically indicates a future alternative in the framework of attempts to study future events rationally. For Bertrand de Jouvenel, who coined the contemporary meaning of the term, the category *futuribles* should only be attributed to "the *futura*, what will be," but "only if its mode of production from the present state of affairs is plausible and imaginable." "A futurible is a *futurum* that appears to the mind as a possible descendant from the present state of affairs." *The Art of Conjecture*, trans. Nikita Lary (New York: Basic Books, 1967),18.

8. Elisa A. Méndez, "Hecho, valor y norma," in *Boletín de la Asociación Argentina de Filosofía del Derecho*, year 8, no. 57, July 1991, 2. From a different methodological perspective, the sociological school emphasizes that "every society gives rise to law and that it corresponds to the norms of organization of any group." Cf. Henri Batiffol, *Filosofía del Derecho* (Buenos Aires: EUDEBA, 1972), 45 ff.

9. Henri Battifol, *Filosofía del Derecho*, 100-101.

10. Alf Ross, *On Law and Justice* (Berkeley: University of California Press, 1959), 280-282. On a different level, Adolfo Gelsi Bidart offers an interesting perspective on justice. ("Aproximación a la Justicia," *Boletín de la Asociación Argentina de Filosofía del Derecho*, year 4, no. 38, 1-3.) He distinguishes between justice of retribution or the correspondence between contributions (commutative justice properly speaking) and justice of acknowledgment of personal status (merits, and virtues, e.g., professional, social, cultural, etc., based on what he calls spirit of justice. He says: "The distinction is brought out well in the parable of the prodigal son. Both sons ask for commutative justice. As the prodigal behaved, so should the father behave. The father, by contrast, aims at justice of acknowledgement. The father behaves as he does because it is his son." The author concludes: "without ceasing to admit and revere justice of retribution or commutative justice, law and social conduct should always seek to revere justice of acknowledgement in family, national, and international spheres. A spirit of justice which a) leaves scales and sword behind, b) rests on the equality of each and every human, c) attempts to personalize the benefit for the other person in the conduct of each individual and of the community as a whole, d) touches every human necessity and interest, e) attempts to extend its inspiration and impulse toward a permanent improvement in the integral human quality of its achievements." Surely, the decision of the father in Gelsi Bidart's felicitous example of the parable of the prodigal son, can only be based on the perfection of the rules of law, a perfection which implicitly carries the attitude of the spirit of justice, just as we propose in our fifth thesis.

11. 320c- 322d. The Argentine edition uses the bilingual version edited by Les Belles Lettres, which is modified by A. Gómez Robledo's interpretation, *Platón: Los seis grandes temas*, 482-483.

12. Antonio Gómez Robledo, *Platón: Los seis grandes temas*, 483, note 17.

13. Plato, *Republic*, 338 c-339 b.

14. Thucydides, *The Peloponnesian War*, V, 105, trans. Rex Warner with intro. and notes by M. I. Finley (London: Penguin Edition, 1954, 1972), 404-455.

15. Jean Baudrillard, "Forget Foucault," 7-64 in *Forget Foucault & Forget Baudrillar: An Interview with Sylvère Lotinger*, Semotex(e) (New York: Foreign Agents Series, Columbia University, 1987), 60.

16. Cf. the appendix on "The Subject and Power" in L. Hubert Dreyfus and Paul Rabinow, *Michel Foucault: Beyond Structuralism and Hermeneutics* (Brighton, Sussex: The Harvester Press, 1982).

17. Cf. "L'oeil du pouvoir," preface to the French translation of Jeremy Bentham, *Le Panoptique* (Paris: Belfond, 1977).

18. Michel Foucault, "Truth and Juridical Forms," 1-89 in *Power*, ed. James D. Faubion, trans. Robert Hurley and others, vol. 3 *Essential Works of Foucault, 1954-1984* (New York: The New Press) 2, 4.

19. To expand on the meaning of this expression, Eric Fromm's *To Have or To Be* is worth consulting (New York: Continuum, 1996): chapter 2 on having and being in daily experience, chapter 4 on the having mode. Fromm's conclusions are based on empirical anthropological and psychoanalytic data and agree with ours.

20. We have taken a similar approach in our study: *La objetividad en ciencias sociales: Un enfoque de epistemología antropológica* (Buenos Aires: Marymar Ediciones, 1987); see especially 50-52.

21. Ludwig Wittgenstein, *Philosophical Investigations*, trans. G. E. M. Anscombe (New York: Macmillan, second edition, 1958), 11 no. 23.

22. Jean-François Lyotard, *The Postmodern Condition: A Report on Knowledge*, trans. Geoff Bennington and Brian Massumi, foreword Frederick Jameson (Minneapolis: University of Minnesota Press, 1984, 1997), chapter 3.

23. Gianni Vattimo, *The Transparent Society*, trans. David Webb (Baltimore: Johns Hopkins University Press, 1992).

24. Ludwig Wittgenstein, *Philosophical Investigations*, 34 no. 71.

25. Ludwig Wittgenstein, *Philosophical Investigations*, 21-23 no. 46-47.

26. Norma Mazzei, *Postmodernidad y narrativa latinoamericana* (Buenos Aires: Ediciones Filofalsía, 1990), 45. This is a clear, useful, very systematic book which responds well to its title.

27. See Jacques Derrida's most important work, *Grammatology*, trans. Gayatri Chakravorty Spivak (Baltimore: Johns Hopkins University Press, 1976).

28. Roland Barthes, *Leçon* (Paris: Seuil, 1978). See Umberto Eco's commentary and criticism in *La estrategia de la ilusión*, (Buenos Aires: Editorial Lumen, Ediciones de la Flor, 1986), chapter entitled "La lengua, el poder, la fuerza." The distinction between power and force (causality) is particularly interesting:

in mass political discourses about power there have been two equivocal phases; the first, naive, in which power had a center. . . . This idea has been sufficiently criticized, and the Foucaultian notion of power arises precisely to show its anthropomorphic naiveté. A trace of this revision of the concept can be found even in the internal contradictions of different terrorist groups. These range from those who want to wound the heart of the state to those, who on the contrary, try to destroy the fabric of power at its periphery, at the points I would call 'Foucaultian,' where the prison official, the small businessman, the foreman operate. The second phase in which force and power are easily confused is more ambiguous. I speak of 'force' instead of causality, which would be my inclination. . . . Let us replace the notion of causality (unidirectional) by force. A force acts upon another force. They form a parallelogram of forces. They do not annul each other, they combine according to a law. The game between forces is reformist. It produces compromise. Yet, the game is never between two forces, but between innumerable forces. . . . To determine what forces are opposed among themselves, certain resolutions intervene which do not depend on the game of forces but on the game of power. A knowledge of the combination of forces results. . . . If we do not reflect sufficiently about this contrast, we fall into different kinds of political infantilism. It is not possible to oppose a force by saying, 'I do not obey you.' Rather, techniques of stopping it are elaborated. But we do not react to a relation of power with a simple, immediate act of force. Power is much more subtle and develops a much more capillary consensus, and heals the wound received, which is always and necessarily at the periphery. Op. *cit.*, 345-348.

29. Dominique Lecourt, *El orden y los juegos. el positivismo lógico cuestionado.* (Buenos Aires: Ediciones de la Flor, 1984), 228.

30. Jean-François Lyotard, *The Postmodern Condition*,10. We will develop this point in the next chapter of our study.

31. Jean-François Lyotard, *The Postmodern Condition*, 10-11.

32. Gianni Vattimo, *The Transparent Society*, 9-11.

33. Cf. Francis Fukuyama, *The End of History and the Last Man* (New York: The Free Press, 1992). Fukuyama's thesis is not original. Its notoriety is surely due to (1) not being directed strictly to the academic world and (2) intending an intelligent legitimation of liberal democracy. Its origin is in the article "The End of History," published in *The National Interest*, no. 16, winter 1989, 21-28.

In the article Fukuyama wonders whether liberal democracy can constitute "the end point of mankind's ideological evolution," "the final form of human government," and whether this would mean the end of history, given that considerable consensus about the legitimacy of liberal democracy as a system of government has arisen in the world." Unlike postmodern authors, Fukuyama's book answers affirmatively the question of whether at the end of the twentieth century it makes sense to speak again about directional, oriented, coherent history which is leading the greater part of humanity toward liberal democracy. The grounding of his thesis rests on an economic interpretation of historical change, which he calls "a logic of modern natural science." Inspired by Hegel's dialectic of master and slave in the *Phenomenology of Spirit*, he remarks (xviii): "The desire for recognition, then, can provide the missing link between liberal economics and liberal politics that was missing from the economic account of History. . . . Desire and reason are together sufficient to explain the process of industrialization, and a large part of economic life more generally. But they cannot explain the striving for liberal democracy, which ultimately arises out of the *thymos* [a direct allusion to Plato], the part of the soul that demands recognition." Fukuyama's intent to sketch the possibility of a new universal history founded in the regulative potentiality of modern natural science and in the desire for recognition, can become for dominant countries an appropriate and even optimistic legitimation discourse which threads together answers to contradictions or at least profound social difficulties of postindustrial neoliberalism. From the approach maintained in our work, we believe that the weakness of Fukuyama's thesis, even accepting all of his presuppositions and the interpretation of history derived from them, is in the belief that liberal principles (based on the conception of freedom and power of having and of domination, respectively) can offer man and society an authentic alternative of being and in the consequent necessity of appealing to irrational forms of *thymos* to complete what the force of these principles would not manage to optimize.

34. Alain Touraine in "Conversación con Alain Touraine," *Revista David y Goliath*, Buenos Aires, CLACSO twentieth anniversary, year 17, no. 52, September, 1987,12.

35. Gianni Vattimo, *The Transparent Society*, 4.

36. Jean Baudrillard, *Seduction*, trans. Bruce Singer (New York: New World Perspectives, 1990), 180-181.

37. Cf. María Cristina Reigadas in "Neomodernidad y posmodernidad: preguntando desde América Latina," in *¿Posmodernidad?* (Buenos Aires: Editorial Biblos, 1988). She describes this characterization of postmodernity (126-129): "I speak of pathos and not of perspective, since the latter implies a certain system, a hunger for order, a point of reference, and a projection which are absent—and even denied—in the postmodern consciousness. Only from outside of it is it valid to speak of perspective. Basically, then the postmodern is a frame of mind, a sensibility, inhabited by multiple artistic, cultural, social, and political movements; an attitude and a mode of experience which cross through and impregnate diverse disciplines, theories, and currents of thought but which does not at all exhaust itself in them."

38. We have elaborated the difference between "expectation" (espera) and "hope" (esperanza) in two studies: *Discépolo: Todavía la esperanza* (Buenos Aires: RundiNuskin Editor, 1990, new enlarged edition, Editorial Almagesto, 1994), where it is one of the central issues of our thesis about Discépolo's work. See also the recorded version of the lecture given in the Fundación Banco de Boston (December 15, 1988), "Las posiblidades de la investigación prospectiva en la Argentina y la cuestión del destino nacional," *Revista E.S.G.*, no. 497, April-June 1990, 87-94.

39. The transvestite (Latin *trans-vestire*, cross-dress) is the one who puts on or disguises himself with different clothing from what he usually uses in order to become unrecognizable. Baudrillard (op. cit., 12-13) perceptively analyzes the subterfuges that drive such behavior, whose similarity with postmodern conduct seems worthy of consideration; especially it might be seen as mirrored by many contemporary "producers" of university knowledge and mass culture. "Transvestism. Neither homosexuals nor transsexuals, transvestites like to play with the indistinctness of the sexes. The spell they cast, over themselves as well as others, is born of sexual vacillation, and not, as is usual, the attraction of one sex for the other. They do not truly like male men or female women, nor those who define themselves, redundantly, as distinct sexual beings. In order for sex to exist, sign must reduplicate biological being. Here the signs are separate from biology, and consequently the sexes no longer exist properly speaking. What the transvestites love is the game of sign, what excites them is *to seduce* the *signs themselves*. With them everything is makeup, theater, seduction. They appear obsessed with games of sex, but they are obsessed first of all with play itself; and if their lives appear more sexually endowed than our own, it is because they make sex into a total, gestural, sensual, and ritual game, an exalted but ironic invocation."

40. Jean-François Lyotard, *The Postmodern Condition*, introduction, xxiii.

41. Jean-François Lyotard, *The Postmodern Condition*, introduction, xxiv.

42. Luis Núñez Ladeveze, "De la utopía clásica a la distopía actual," en *Revista de Estudios Políticos* (Madrid: Centro de Estudios Constitucionales), no. 44, new series, March-April 1985,47

43. Luis Núñez Ladeveze, op. cit., 68.

44. Paul Ricoeur, *Lectures on Ideology and Utopia* (New York: Columbia University Press, 1986). This excellent book publishes eighteen lectures edited by George H. Taylor, delivered at the University of Chicago during fall 1975. Following Mannheim and with characteristic acuteness, Paul Ricoeur examines the concepts of ideology and utopia. "The organizing hypothesis is that the very conjunction of these two opposite sides or complementary functions typifies what could be called social and cultural imagination" (1). Authors analyzed are Marx, Althusser, Mannheim, Weber, Habermas, Geertz, Saint-Simon, and Fourier.

45. Gianni Vattimo, *The Transparent Society*, 71

46. Rafael Angel Herra, op. cit., 158. These two poles of knowledge in the field of ideology and specifically in culture, sciences, and philosophy are for Herra "what refers to its meaning (from an immanent view) and what refers to its function (from an extrinsic viewpoint in reference to the content of the theory). Meaning constitutes the paradigm of determinations of the system. The function of this field of meaning is its application, its practice" (ibidem). In 1984 this essay represented the first critical reflection in Costa Rica about the problem of violence. On 91-94 the author formulated the relation, "human rights and utopia." In this regard we select the following passage which coincides with our position, but about which we have not pronounced ourselves in the body of the present investigation:

> human rights are not only the utopia of the future. Their paradox consists in that they are today the only utopia that is being built and is in process, which takes root and which gives its teleology to what ought to be. Normative here does not only mean that in positive law man has been declared formally and legally free or with rights to work, to culture, and to a livable environment. What is important is that it orients his action, projects reasons in the present struggle. Rights are values, postulates, normative ideals, partial realizations which peoples have gradually achieved and which are still far from completion and even from final formulation. If, unhappily, the men of the future produce unforeseen conditions of repression, the utopia of new rights which are also unforeseen today will be raised against them.

47. Cf. George Orwell, *1984* (New York: Signet, 1949); Aldous Huxley, especially his utopia *Island: a Novel* (New York: Harper, 1962); B. F. Skinner, *Walden Two* (New York: Macmillan, 1948) and *Beyond Freedom and Dignity*, (New York: Knopf, 1971).

48. Jean-François Lyotard, *The Postmodern Condition*, introduction, 14.

49. Jean-François Lyotard, *The Postmodern Condition*, introduction, 46.

50. "Entrevista con Burrhus Frederic Skinner," in *Las utopías* (Barcelona: Salvat Editores, 1973, Text by José María Carandell.

51. Jean-François Lyotard, *The Postmodern Condition*, introduction, 40.

52. Jean-François Lyotard, *The Postmodern Condition*, introduction, 41.

Chapter 8

The Sense of What Is to Come

1. The Experience of Power and Freedom

It is not our intention to construct a preview of what is to come from futuribles that we have analyzed during our investigation. The title, "Sense of What Is to Come" indicates that our study is an attempt to deepen a reflection about the direction events are taking. In fact, the basic present tendencies will in all probability be maintained. What is not yet clear and what cannot be the subject of agreement is whether the processes under way have a definite goal. We feel that what is in doubt is not the existence of some finality. Obviously, even the ab= surd or the casual has a sense. But setting aside this claim, which we have not proved, it is evident that the question we pose is not initially cosmological but anthropological. It depends on us and concerns our "world," that is, the symbolic world in which we are situated and which we form by the daily exercise of our freedom.

Examples of the basic tendencies that already shape events are the adoption of a new logic which brings with it the transformation of paradigms of homogeneity and unidirectional causality into new paradigms of the heterogeneity of social products and multicausality in sciences; the universal acceptance of the technology of cybernetics and of communications in almost every discipline and in daily life; or the development of genetics and genetic engineering. It is already true that there is an increasing awareness of the necessity of a less partial and frivolous philosophical, legal, and social evaluation of the impact of technological "progress." It is no less certain that when this effort does not include the legitimation of the type of society and knowledge that the phenomena seem to

105

carry with them, it is usually deflected or discredited by a counterattack complaining of opposition to change. Its spokesmen are denounced as regressive representatives of an alleged metaphysical tradition. So for philosophy to bring the response of human engagement and to uncover an implicit teleology, it still must be acknowledged as an inevitable, anthropological alternative which can awaken us from the alienation of opting for the direction demanded by instinct. Because if there is something about which philosophers do not doubt, it is that reality is not simply something there and that reality can give rise to many metaphors. However, the human temptation to remain in one instrumental configuration of reality has demolished all philosophical critique and instead encouraged irrational fears along with the fantasy that man could overcome the metaphysical uncertainty of existence through the extension of his instinct in the domination of gods, nature, and other men. Therefore, reality has generally taken the historical form of universal metaphors (organism, macrocosm, machine) which permit us to identify ourselves with what we experience as threat. The interpretation that has been made of human ontological freedom as psychological freedom and of its power of historical realization as the power of domination reveals this psychological mimetic process engendered by existential insecurity. Furthermore, this is the principal thesis which has inspired our whole investigation. If both levels of freedom and power are not profoundly distinguished, any presentation of this sort of power will be an ideological or eristic exhibition, as in the worst sort of sophistic.

Albert Einstein once affirmed: *"The true value of a human being* is determined primarily by the measure and sense in which he has attained the liberation from self."[1] That assertion connects with wisdom of both East and West, and properly understood permits us to recognize that our own humanity can only be found when we go a step beyond a look in the mirror. We believe that the future of mankind engages all of us in a special way. Only through the gaze of the other can we effectively recognize ourselves as identity and open a space of the authentic freedom of being, which makes us grow in lucidity. So we reject ethnocentric approaches, whether open like modernity, or contrived like postmodernity. When modern man decided to retake a place in the world and construct more reliable knowledge, he tried the route of focusing on himself but almost instantly found himself without a world. Then he had to construct from the exterior in the illusion that he projected his own universe. Human history from modernity to the present eloquently exhibits that ego which cloaks itself with the being of reality to appropriate it with greater efficacy. This process of constituting the configuring subject of the world paradoxically dissolves into the exterior character of the model. As a dystopic specimen of modernity's project, postmodernity expresses the crisis of the experience of freedom.

We have seen that the experience of freedom and power is the very history of man considered in terms of the capacity of meaning. The crisis of the idea of history occurs because we are submerged in a crisis of meaning. Power as the temporal realization of freedom only actualizes its meanings. Freedom of doing or of having has shown us its horizon of possibilities for man: to continue deepening the path of alienation attired in the delights of the kingdom of utility and to submit ourselves to the seduction of the spaces of domination power, conquered at the cost of permanent disenchantment. The social sciences account for this *external* experience of freedom and power. However, the perspectives of the future movement of this experience seem to go in another direction. The present, exotic, individualist, and syncretistic turn toward pseudo-religious, spiritual circles, which have characterized periods of historical crises, though products of that same psychological freedom, already constitute the first fruits of a fracture. The necessity of men to encounter a new framework of reference, a new horizon of sense in which they can establish bonds with a broader and more genuine rationality, is the breaking point. The key to the possibility is in our capacity to give new meaning originating from our ontological freedom

Therefore, we think that coming decades will specially manifest humanity's interest in the metaphysical dimension of life. This interest will be the cause of social and cultural transformations even more profound than those that will continue in the scientific, technological domain.

2. Philosophy of Law and Postmodernity

Lyotard judges that postmodern development puts a decisive factor in the foreground: scientific praxis, with its denotative propositions, demands rules, or in other words, prescriptive or metaprescriptive propositions. These rules are prescriptions in the manner of axiomatic systems: "they prescribe what the moves in language games must be to be admissible."[2] The scientific language game is just another game. But is it truly one game among others? Amid much abstract glitter, an obscure point continues to be the truth-effect of scientific propositions, what we used to call the semantic question. In social praxis, theories function as truths and models operate as the *substance* of reality, since they signify persons' lives, reveal meanings, and confer effective rewards and punishments, namely toward further development or isolation. What perspectives does law have in the framework of this scheme? Is it inscribed as the science game or constituted from social praxis? Are freedom, social order, and justice matters of law? Or can they be referred to an admissible paradigm? In the latter case, is power regulated by law or does the power of the strongest impose criteria of regulation? It is evident that there are no operative rules empty of meaning. Nominalism is also metaphysics. Scientific nominalism is much more so, since it seeks the effect of ideologies without their utopian component.

Undoubtedly, law arises by and for life in society. It finds its objects in bonds that men establish. These bonds express a horizon of meanings: expectations and hopes, traditions and values. But the social practice that configures these relations does not have the simplicity of the sciences: "It is a monster formed by the intertwining of various networks of heteromorphous classes of utterances (denotative, prescriptive, performative, technical, evaluative etc.)."[3] Does law therefore play the science game or is it another type of game? How do we recognize the spirit of justice, if ontological freedom is excluded from considerations by knowledge? Can the desire of justice be satisfied by the postulation of a system coherence principle? We always return to Thrasymachus. However, the reason of the strongest is not the argument. We now have performative truth (as better actuation of the metanarrative of scientific, technological knowledge).

For Lyotard the legitimation of the social bond cannot come from the notion of "universal consensus" as Habermas proposes—a "universal," moreover, that could only come out of Europe and "its *own* traditions," which have "the penetration, the energy, the will, and the imagination" to do it.[4] In place of that, following the scientific model, Lyotard suggests, "any consensus on the rules defining a game and the 'moves' playable within it *must* be local, in other words agreed upon by the present players and subject to eventual cancellation. The orientation favors a multiplicity of finite meta-arguments, by which I mean argumentation that concerns metaprescriptives and is limited in space and time."[5] In other words, a "temporary contract" replaces the permanence of human bonds and the stability of the institutions that sustain them. Allowing this does not mean we are emancipated from the egotism of the slaves of power nor that we are opened to personalizing encounters of cultures. When the spaces of non-hegemonic identity are reduced to expressions of finite narratives, they lack legitimacy to universalize their will to being, because the horizon of the future already has paradigms supported by the advanced industrial societies' technological truths. The point of view of Habermas differs from the approach of Lyotard in that the former still trusts in the recuperation of modern reason and in the renewing of certain values converted in the "grimace of domination." The latter would dispose spirits for performative "possession" based on a heteromorphism of language games and on the social assumption (which contradicts the results of scientific knowledge) of the *inevitable* continuity of tendencies in progress.

Social interaction thought of as pragmatic linguistics, as language games, operates as the evolution of discontinuities, where tradition no longer functions as conservator of the spaces of freedom and belonging that have been achieved by man. Tradition, and with it law and history, are dissolved in a time without intentionality and without interiority. The past does not exist, and the future is exhausted in every play. Man thus loses his historicity.

At the inception of Enlightenment critique, "authority" is converted into a "source of prejudices," alien to the act of recognition and cognition upon which it rests, and its notion is deformed by being opposed to reason and freedom. "The concept of tradition however," Gadamer explains,[6]

> has become no less ambiguous than that of authority, and for the same reason—namely that what determines the romantic understanding of tradition is its abstract opposition to the principles of enlightenment. . . . The fact is that in tradition there is always an element of freedom and of history itself. Even the most genuine and pure tradition does not persist because of the inertia of what once existed. It needs to be affirmed, embraced, cultivated. It is, essentially, preservation, and it is action in all historical change. Never-

theless, preservation is an act of reason, although characterized by the fact that it does not call attention to itself. For this reason only innovation and planning appear to result from reason. But this is an illusion. Even where life changes most violently, as in ages of revolution, far more of the old is preserved in the supposed transformation of everything than anyone knows, and it combines with the new to create a new value. At any rate, preservation is a conduct that is as much free action as revolution and renewal. That is why both the Enlightenment critique of tradition and the romantic rehabilitation of tradition lag behind their true historical being.

If history is not the source of possibilities of the future, and the present is emptied of historicity and of the feeling of a future which has taken root as the expression of identity of a people, what is a philosophy of law for? Will it be possible to effectively respect desires for justice, as Lyotard augurs in the last paragraph of his report on the postmodern condition? Or will only the game of "small narratives" which do not alter the equilibrium of the system be permitted? If we discount metaphysical questions and with them philosophical interrogatives, man will see himself as a finite possibility in an *environment*—not in a world—which determines him. His freedom, even freedom of choosing, will be analogous to the freedom of a variable within a system: its role defined in the "social environment" and the probabilities of its behavior and of its interactions also determined, its life trajectory able to be simulated. Certainly this has been the project of "the positivist 'philosophy' of efficiency."[7] However, contrary to Lyotard, it is also the spirit that the postmodern narrative retains when anarchy, innovation, imagination, and paralogism hope to be included, if not as new measurable and controllable alternatives in the manner of the positive search for efficiency, then as sure discontinuities, which do not modify the great language game of the power of domination.

Only God does not do metaphysics. As long as man does not cease to be an ontologically dissatisfied, incomplete finitude, interrogatives of a metaphysical nature will unsettle his existence and open paths at the cost of the crises of narratives. In the face of the challenge of the future of man, if philosophy of law is not to waste its best opportunities as mere "chronicle of ideas" or "speculative accounting," a completely neutralized "knowledge of law," it ought again to be understood as philosophy and attain the possibility of thinking about man in interaction with other men. In the last analysis, men are the "necessary creators" of norms which channel their aspirations for freedom and also order power as freedom's concretion.

As Gadamer clearly demonstrates,[8] it is meaningless to speak of complete knowledge of history, since historical being is not exhausted when it is known. The pretension to a "science of law" that could contain the complete knowledge of law itself (including its ground) is also useless. Philosophers of law are currently concerned to ratify the variations of power and freedom in a sort of logical system, and contumaciously resist accepting as *questions*—in our acceptation of the term—the ethical, metaphysical interrogatives that underlie any legal ordering. This only facilitates the legitimation of the project of homogenization of knowledge and the new universalization of the dystopia of control by the "deciders." We insist that homogeneity is produced at the expense of heterogeneity, only tolerated as the atomization and relativization of knowledge and culture. Other periods planned to suppress discontinuities in disparate cultural loyalties by acknowledging a clear and distinct reason which operated without errors of the desires of will. Now, in the impossibility of suppressing outbursts of the freedom of being which express the ontological richness of the cultural heterogeneity of each people, homogeneity is sought by way of the internalization of a shared universal destiny in the mode of a shared metanarrative capable of sustaining the meaning of the legitimating narratives of each culture.

Law is knowledge whose positive content has roots in the historicity of the social subject's behavior. The plenitude of its manifestation is the spread of the spirit of justice in human exchanges. The philosophy of law in future society has its own field: to smooth the path with new alternative horizons of meaning for the achievement of a legal order in which justice according to Thrasymacus would be only a moment in the consciousness of humanity. Is this possible? The *future* of the philosophy of law depends on our capacity to assume and construct the future history *now*. We refer to a philosophy of law which has abandoned the game of passive legitimation of the projects of the dominative power within some particular order; and to a philosophy of law which anticipates the sense of a power of achievement in which persons and peoples discover themselves in their search for infinity from the roots of man's ontological freedom. Far from postulating the utopia of a perfect society, we want to situate ourselves in the particular tension of existence itself and, with its movement of transcendence, elevate ourselves to the lucidity of a fuller human life.

Notes

1. Albert Einstein, *The World As I See It* (New York: Covici, Friede Publishers, 1934), 245.

2. Jean-François Lyotard, *The Postmodern Condition*: *A Report on Knowledge*, trans. Geoff Bennington and Brian Massumi (Minneapolis, University of Minnesota Press, 1984, 1997), 65.

3. Lyotard, *The Postmodern Condition*, 65.

4. Jürgen Habermas, *The Philosphical Discourse of Modernity, Twelve Lectures*, trans. Frederick G. Lawrence (Cambridge, Mass.: MIT Press, 1987, 1996), 432-433.

5. Lyotard, *The Postmodern Condition*, 66.

6. Hans-Georg Gadamer, *Truth and Method*, trans. Jack Weinsheimer and Donald G. Marshall (New York: Crossroad, second revised edition, 1989), 281-282.

7. Lyotard, *The Postmodern Condition*, 54.

8. Gadamer, *Truth and Method*. 298.

Chapter 9

Postmodern Metanarrative as Transvestite Logic

Postmodernity characterizes or at least accounts for our historic circumstance. It has been amply described by thinkers and critics of varied disciplines and cultural backgrounds. Despite diverse and even mutually contradictory interpretations, its planetary impact is not in doubt. Some of the features of this description have almost achieved the status self-evident assumptions of any reflection on the phenomenon. One such assumption is precisely the universality of postmodernism.

However, these commonplaces need to be considered from a different critical perspective. It is useful to start by insisting that postmodernity cannot be fully comprehended without being situated in relation to postindustrialism. We must keep in mind how telecommunications and cybernetics involve a qualitative change in traditional industrial production because of the strategic importance of information and knowledge in order to adequately judge postmodernity, the reverse of the postindustrial spiritual coin.

In the dense and complex contemporary debate about postmodernity, the principal thesis is the claim about "the crisis of grand narratives." Leading theorists hold the apocalyptic view that postmodernity is the *end of history*, the loss of a unitary sense of history. Former legitimating metanarratives lack efficacy, whether they are modernity's story of emancipation or idealism's speculative tale. Today there are a variety of small narratives, which we can picture as linguistic games. For example, science is one language game among others. These games find their legitimation in themselves. Social interaction is articulated by the linguistic praxis which determines the rules which the subjects who participate in a particular game or determined social practice must follow. Moreover,

111

human subjects determine meanings in this pragmatic situation. It is not strange to find the hypothesis that there are as many meanings as interpreters.

From a complementary perspective, the postmodern can be said to express a crisis of anxiety about a model of rationality that grounds human life, being, and acting, a model which does not contain man or exceeds his comprehension of the direction of the changes under way, and which has shown on its face evident signs of contradiction in its practical realization. This crisis is manifested at all levels and is marked by the importance of the fragmentary, the provisional, the syncretism of forms, the crude, and the simulated as correlative of technocratic, industrial society which is highly sophisticated in the double sense of being artificial and complicated in its refinement.

Philosophical consideration of postmodernity from Latin America offers analytic elements which permit an interpretation substantially different from those customary in the debate.

a. Postmodernity is not abandonment of great narratives nor the end of history. To the contrary, it attempts to initiate a new narrative, a new evaluation of history, which profoundly affects social bonds and subtly conditions possibilities of being and the capacity to react on one's own, to universalize the identity of the people of Latin America and of other non-hegemonic societies.

The great narrative of postmodernity springs from the metanarrative of modernity that it replaces. It is its substitute. Specifically, it expresses not the crisis of the contemporary world, but the crisis of central societies. At bottom this is an endogenous crisis occurring within postindustrial societies. Therefore, it is not *per se* a planetary crisis.

b. At the heart of the crisis, all reality seems to be affected. But it is worth pointing out that "the reality" mentioned has a taste for imperious, modern, universal reason which has consumed other possible worlds. The very fact that it affects *us* profoundly reveals not only the matrix of relations of dependence which link us to that center, but also the spirit of domination which it exercises even when it doubts its efficacy, without even considering the contemporary phenomenon of the impact of the mass media. Accordingly, the present point of view is different from that of typical participants in the postmodernism debate. The latter maintain that postmodernity breaks with modernity or that it perverts and betrays it.[1] I take it rather that postmodernity is the result or culmination of modernity, but I draw quite different conclusions from those of other exponents of this point of departure.

c. In reality, the new narrative perfects the operability of the instrumental, ethnocentric rationality of European modernity.

That focus marks the difference between my perspective and that of European and North American thinkers. What may have lost executive capacity and operative efficacy is precisely that rationality that based its whole operation on the ideal of reason or that rationality which articulated a particular meaning of historical events. This is not to deny that other, alternative discourses might exist or be sought which similarly legitimate the paradigmatic role of certain societies, and certain peoples in history. The main difference in relation to modernity is that new appeals to grounding renounce metaphysical and ethical principles which used to justify the practical universalization of hegemonic projects.

Now the recourse is to legitimating principles without the taint of moral conscience, because evidently this reduces efficacy in acting by posing contradictions between principles and aspirations to the power of domination. Consequently, one (like Lyotard for example) asks where to find the new legitimation when the force of the great narratives has been lost.

d. Asking this is strange and even hypocritical. It implies accepting a certain type of narrative which justifies as a universal phenomenon what one hides in particular cases (with pretenses). There will be no end to grand narratives but a need to reformulate them to make them more efficacious.

In other words, without abandoning certain constitutive grounds of the modern metanarrative, postmodern thinkers implicitly or explicitly hold a kind of irreversible direction of events. It is a different manner of maintaining the idea of progress, a reedition of the idea which inspired earlier speculation. Irreversibility in the direction of events now refers to the development of the knowledge and activity characteristic of postindustrial societies, heirs of the old historical subjects. Their mode of social interaction, a product of technical knowledge and computerized information, inspires the underlying axiology of postmodern culture.

e. The idea of historical progress freed from the bonds of morality subsists. Therefore, the space of power can develop in an infinite space of tonalities (marginal cultures and nonhegemonic societies) whose only identifying characteristic, as Wittgenstein might say, is the nonsense of their *little* games of emancipatory narratives.

The grand new narrative of postmodernity takes the form of *the ideal of operative reason*. This ontology of better acting has two objectifying facets: to optimize efficiency and stress success. In a nutshell, it exalts externality with a hyperrealism of forms.

The essence of efficiency is, first, to postulate the autonomy of science. (Despite being just another linguistic game, science is set up as the criterion of the normative authority for other language games.) Second, it postulates axiological independence of technological progress (whose propositions function as the result of truth, though not exactly in the epistemological sense).

f. In this interpretation, what I call "transvestite logic" constitutes the mode in which the new metanarrative is set up. The metanarrative's object is to sustain the basic ties of power of domination and circumscribe the potentiality of the realization of narratives in dependent communities.

This logic is labeled "transvestite" because it works by the employment of a mechanism of simulation by signs, a pure "game of signs," in Baudrillard's expression.[2] It simultaneously hides and exhibits disinterest in life and fascination *with consumption and technological power without, however, revealing* the totalitarian will which inspires the metanarrative. Its effect is to disassociate the axiological and historical commitment of local narratives (Lyotard) and their aspirations to identity and freedom of being. What is personal is dissolved into individual vacuums. Private life is stripped of interiority, without communicational and expressive networks other than the reflection of the world of images.

1. Beyond Habermas and Lyotard, or Perhaps in Spite of Them

a. Is it possible to "live standing tall"? This might be the anthropological question of our time. Hope, elementary confidence in being and existing, is placed in doubt. Human relations in all of life are upset.

The sense of existence, not just of personal existence but of humanity''s, is the object of controversy, of market calculation, or of disputes that express our narcissism. It has ceased to be an assumption upon which opinions about our destiny take issue with one another.

b. History has become recurring. We have entered the cycle of hysteresis. "We have no choice but to accept that there is no longer an end, that there will be no end." We are dead, "we live" the illusion of the world. Baudrillard concludes amending Zarathrustra. Still, Baudrillard is a prolific writer.

Chaos, destruction, final stages of inertia, a metastatic state—the catastrophic has devoured the meaning of the apocalyptic. The state of things we live no longer *reveals* anything. In any case, it only shows that "which, like nails or hair, continues to grow after death."[3]

Accused of ignorance and skeptical bad faith by his contemporaries, the popular Buenos Aires poet Enrique Santos Discépolo was far from any game of simulation. He still had confidence in the recuperation of reason as a value and as "mental health." His 1935 lyrics for the tango *Cambalache* anticipate the situation we analyze:[4]

> *Igual que en la vidriera irrespetuosa*
> *de los cambalaches*
> *se ha mezclado la vida.*
> *Y herido por un sable sin remache*
> *ves llorar la Biblia contra un calefón.*

Differentiating between the two experiences of the world is essential to evaluate what initially appears to be a comparable critical discourse, which in its turn would permit the object of the comparison to be manifested. Any external or formal analogy neutralizes comprehension of what has been understood to produce an absolutely nonexistent uniformity of experiences. Precisely, the difference does not rest on an intellectual account of the crisis of reason or whether or not "we enter beyond history upon pure fiction, . . . on to *the greatly more radical illusion of the world.*"[5]

c. To privilege discursive logic, particularly discourse about the meaning of our place in the world, which is what we are discussing, is to hide what is fundamental, the ground where these lived experiences find their possibility of being and objectifying themselves in language. Otherwise, we let ourselves be seduced by an abstract, undifferentiated universality stripped of any pathos. But the spiritual state of cryogenesis or hysterisis is really a product packaged in social imagery and marketed by interested parties. It need not be the only social paradigm. (Do we not assume we float on the confusion and implosion of values?) Whether paradigm or rather new *paradogm*, obviously, even when flesh and blood humans are overdetermined by pressure of this imagery and practically incapable of reacting against its impositions, they will never cease to suffer the tension of freedom without metaphors, the inevitable freedom of responding to what our existence asks. If life did not have the specific dimension of questions for us[6] (I include Baudrillard in this game), what would this urge to produce postmillennial affirmations matter? Pronouncements about definitive accomplishments while we wallow in the ephemeral are paradoxical. Regarding the paradox, perhaps Wittgenstein's question is worth remembering: "But is it possible for one so to live that life stops being problematic? That one is living in eternity and not in time?"[7] Accordingly, my reflection stresses that the different perspectives found in Baudrillard and Discépolo are comparable to a dialogue between what might be called "the game of satisfied irony" and "the dramatic game of hope sustained against the evanescence of daily expectations." The difference is between the vacuum which occurs when a limit has been exceeded and the pain caused by an assent to life whose ontological horizon has been truncated, a kind of North-South division of human existence.

d. Baudrillard informs us that we can only hope. This distinguishes him from Lyotard. The inevitability of progress has been modified by the force of progress itself into the prolongation of death which has already occurred. Only awareness (?) of delusion, the possibility of rendering history poetically would be left. Yet, is this poetry merely free on bail? Is it an ecstasy of words due to mere linguistic seduction? Is it aesthetic onanism? What does it matter unless it involves some claim that life has sense?[8] Indeed, without an apocalypse, catastrophe becomes anastrophe by the inversion of meaning. However, these descriptions show not just a state of mind but also a rational, aesthetic, and moral (!) effort to establish the inevitable direction of events (as in Lyotard but with different arguments). We cross or have already crossed over the bridge which takes us from an apology for individualism encouraging innovative ruptures because it assumed temporal progress, and inevitably arrive at the vacuum of narcissist atemporality.[9] As happens elsewhere, we end by confusing liberty and absence of limits.

e. For Discépolo, and with him everyone for whom the limit of satisfaction, of abundance, is still "a wide and strange world," there is no place for "estheticizing hyperreality."[10] Life is pathos above all, and therefore possibility even if possibility in the desert. Delusions are part of the landscape which the desert path offers, projections of expectations which consume licit or illicit results. However, the desert cannot be crossed without hope. Hope makes our expectations succeed each other without abandoning life. One can only die standing up when one has lived standing up. Real, profound America accepts change, but refuses to fly without roots. It wants to, and can, see with its own eyes. So I ask whether that desert ought to be emptiness and indifferentiation for Latin America?

In moments of vigorous modernist conviction, Europe already saw an empty space in which to develop its own civilizing rationality. But the empty space was not a desert. It was not a blank page. The barbarians also had their gods. At the turn of the twenty-first century that civilizing rationality imposes a barbarism without gods. The old enlightened or emancipatory metanarrative was universal and exclusive. The goal was there, and here were *the* means. Its optimism ended in awareness of tragedy, its utopia in dystopia. One of the visible faces of postmodernity is sorrowful. What is not so clear is that its sorrow ought to drag us once again into a similarly universal, exclusive narrative.

f. Lyotard and Habermas, two of the principle participants in the modernity-postmodernity debate, present a paradigmatic revision of the ancient family disagreement regarding the monopoly of reason. Despite them, however, the sphere of *the other*, marginalized in the dispute or made an object of desire, does exist. Whether as antitotalizing thought (Lyotard) or reconciling thought (Habermas) we find that the schematism of center and periphery continues to be legitimated. Epistemological obsession with fragmentation or unity leaves no effective conversion of spirits but the inversion of market logic. That logic adapts to an *Idea*, which foundered in the arms of Parmenides, and a Light, which managed to erase the outlines of difference. Both are products of the rationality which shows the impact of arrogant autonomy. If, previously, *the other* was a desert which had to be made fertile by the progress of reason or the development of freedom, now it is a democratic space authorized for local narratives, restricted games. This means that the logic of thought has not achieved a Copernican revolution. New philosophical screeds or in their place voluptuous literary gyrations affirm that our reality is still unreal. Historically submerged in fragments of modern *episteme*, we are allowed to live the nonsense of the present in terms of the deconstruction of postmodern *episteme*. What is certain is the plantetary establishment of the phenomenon called postmodernism, like it or not. Therefore, from the perspective of those who do not make the basic rules of the possible games, we seek out the argument about *meaning* in the era of emptiness.

2. The Inheritance or about the Discovery
of the Land of Dystopia

g. If we were really permeated by meaninglessness and if our lives were restricted to the eternity of the instant or to a single desire with a powerful emotional impact (a corporeal, permissive version of the Cartesian cogito), we would not waste time producing so much literature or so much discourse about postmodernity's reality or lack thereof.

Language appears when mediation is necessary. Without his mirror Narcissus is not even an artificial idea. We who aspire to be professional thinkers are accustomed to resounding claims about the end of history, the last man, the era of emptiness, the lightness of being, the end of metanarratives, and sundry catastrophic or mischievous expressions that are put on the market for the consumption of intellectuals and the scandal of the profane who do not understand the simulation games to which we are accustomed. The expressions encourage an illegitimate prophetic mode which seeks to gain a space of power and acknowledgment, bringing enlightenment out of confusion by a discourse which complements modernity's. Exaltation of chaos can only be expressed from an order in which that chaos is contained (or tries to be contained). For example, the announcement of the death of God is unimaginable without another human ideal, that of the superman, which personifies the value of life. From a traditional logical perspective the only coherent behavior in the face of the lack of being would be to allow oneself to die. Assuming that we renounce man's propensity for meaning, is it possible to imagine any language other than mere fiction or more properly silence, from the perspective of a logic which proclaims the absence of seriousness of the world? It is not possible! As Discépolo told us, what is unacceptable from any point of view is discourse legitimating an axiological kaleidoscope, a lack of coherence: to proclaim a sort of liberating nihilism, the practical acceptance of "anything goes," but then faced with the effective, the real, not the theoretical manifestation of that nihilism in terrorism and genetic, social, or ecological violence, to demand the rights of a rationality that was absent from the assumptions which guided the discourse of thinkers beyond good and evil. The simulation of unwanted disciples pursues Nietzsche. Doubtless the last thing one can expect from thought in this situation is an appeal to a finality or counterfinality of the world, or to the becoming of the subject or of the object, or even to the language of seduction.

h. However, I can envisage a more consistent argument in favor of meaninglessness. Baudrillard is the spokesman of the view that "We are, then, unable to dream of a past or future state of things. Things are in a state which is literally definitive—neither finished, or infinite, but de-finitive, that is, deprived of its end."[11]

From the simulation logic in which postmodern thinkers situate themselves, no desire of the subject is anything but a projection of the seductive game of the object. Excluding the desire for God, condemning the utopia of autonomous reason's good judgment, with the luminous progress of conscience asphyxiated at Auschwitz, we are left with the pathetic game of monstrous, sinister objects. We are left with the artifacts of modernity's desire (the freedom to have, and the power to dominate), which today are no more than an effluvium of the exercise of our freedom to configure the world.

But if I have to take seriously this description of the state of affairs in which we humans are immersed, beyond Baudrillard's satisfied irony, I still must ask: What is the point of revealing this enjoyment, this savoring, this express desire to dispose of the end, to exhaust and attend the final spectacle described to us, to discover in it the truth about the question of man, the answers about meaning, to finally unveil the class of game to which we are called in this life with the cards on the table. Is not this human vocation, curiosity, or sickness incoherent or at least strange: to find the meaning of life when one affirms, whether as a simulation or not, that everything is already definitive? Longing for meaning would seem to reject both the impossibility of dreaming the literal evidence of the end and the literal evidence of the origin. It challenges us to doubt the nightmares that we construct. Tellingly, if we confine the overdone discourse of postmodern thinkers and come to grips with the radical exercise of philosophical thought, even if the strategies of the object surpass the subject's understanding,[12] they cannot silence the interrogatives about meaning that spring from the experience of the finitude of existence. Even in its most perverse form of theory, the very object gives us back the possibility of lucidity, which is always partial and momentary, about the ontological ambiguity of human existence. It frees us from the veils of psychological security to which inevitable legitimations subject us by the mere fact of being human. It puts us in the presence of the moment of the radical finitude that we are, which even as a simple spectator is incapable of resigning itself to its nothingness, to the death of every dream of infinity.

i. It is healthy to note that these dreams of infinity are not the result of metaphysics, however its discourse is constructed. The metaphysical question has its root in the tension of human existence's ambiguity. But this question deserves separate treatment. It is astonishing that contemporary thought still aligns itself with positivism against metaphysics because of the crass error of identifying these interrogatives with specific modes of doing metaphysics in the history of western thought. It is surprising that distinguished thinkers from different speculative positions strive to avoid the slightest taint of a formal tie to that tradition, although to substitute for it, they elaborate similar argumentation and terminology under the imperative of a quasi-Platonic "going beyond" metaphysics.

Man is a finite being with aspirations to infinity, that is, to meaning and fulfillment, even when he despairs of this finality or thinks he knows that there is no finality. The possibility of the absurdity of life is an issue which envelops the most dramatic experience of the interrogative about meaning. At this point, at the start of any narrative, meaninglessness is eliminated as an original alternative of existence. Only through the mediation of the thematization of the interrogative, can meaninglessness, nothingness, or the vacuum become a possibility and engage me as an answer. But by themselves, this nothingness, this lack of weight of being, are clearly not the manifestation of an original fact of existence, but the result of the exercise of my personal freedom to give meaning to the world, one legitimating objectification among others of my position toward the interrogative of existence.

j. Yet does not postmodernity unveil the fictitious meaning humanity has claimed up to now? Do postmodern thinkers surprise us by taking their post on the cultural landscape as crusaders for "the" truth which the masters of suspicion present, limiting themselves to gloss and describe voluptuously the details of a prophecy which has come true? Or perhaps do we simply feel impotence because of the lack of adequate responses to a state of crisis?

As a game,[13] postmodernity clearly represents the state of culture in the postindustrial period. Labels that indicate certain common classifications are frequently weapons that exempt those who use them from examining the content of the labels. Still, postmodernity and postindustrialism are phenomena which coincide within the same type of society, the kind of society to which both Bell and Habermas belong. Ideological groupings do not facilitate the understanding of the situation. Rather, a dispassionate analysis of the several discourses will get us closer to what is occurring in a seemingly endless oscillation in the postmodern spirit between having no finality and opening up future spaces of marvels (projected hyperindustrialism). For what is manifested in the game of representing the postmodern phenomenon? Is Vattimo[14] right in saying that the end of European domination (an expression equivalent to "the end of history"), the criticism of modernity, and the advent of mass media have granted a voice to local cultures and minorities? What kind of voice is allowed? Above all, how? In what communicational context is it situated? If we agree with Lyotard in supporting Wittgenstein's theory that there are a plurality of linguistic uses, the word has sense only in the game in which it appears, that is, in the vertigo of mass media driven by interests of great international corporations. Could this scenario satisfy the concerns of Alain Touraine[15] about the complete divorce between society and actors observable at the turn of the millennium, where neo-liberalism and postmodernism coexist? One describes a society reduced to a market without actors, while the other imagines actors without a system, enclosed in their imagination and memories. Might not a connecting thread for a new legitimation that concerns Lyotard be found here?

k. Many observers have claimed that the very name postmodernity is contradictory. Rather, it seems potentially helpful. It can orient us on the quest for a response, even if partial and open, to some of the interrogatives we have posed. Obviously, the name depends on a whole historical definition. Though the postmodern movement is primarily and variously a break with historicism, the prefix "post" does emphasize a turning point in the historical project of modernity. But it does not constitute a break with its basic conception. The name, which is not arbitrary, maintains continuity with the liberty of doing or having, whose factual reality is the power of domination. This freedom shapes modernity's ontological horizon, whose argument is anticipated in the sixteenth century in the first fruits of the encounter with the other world in "the greatest genocide in human history."[16]

If postmodernity really implied the break with the cultural and intellectual tradition that many scholars claim, we would not find ourselves in a state of confusion and retreat entrenched in hedonism and hyperindividualism. Schizoid behavior would not be the model of social practice.

Furthermore, the observation that there is a dissociation between the public and the private or more exactly a complete separation between instrumentality and meaning, only confirms that we are at a turning point in the roots of the very process. The turning point represents the end of a tendency, but not a break with it.

The phenomenon takes the form of a dystopia, a bad place, in which modernity's *utopia* of (instrumental) Reason and Freedom (of appropriation) carried out their ambition to be in the world. In reality, the contrasts, public and private and instrumentality and meaning, found their deepest legitimation in the thought of modernity. They served the purpose of elaborating theories which allowed the civilizing conquest of nature, including in the latter the peoples whom the good use of reason anointed with progress.

l. Nevertheless, postmodernity can be said to be the end of a history. It ends the history of a rationality which abolished every dream but showed a certain efficacy for accomplishing dreams. This omnipotent rationality ultimately submerged us in the deep pit of every dream, Discépolo's "neutral gear of souls," the game of delusion and agony which wear down hope. In this game we go from expectation to expectation in the demand for the immediate satisfaction of desire, in the loneliness of an instrumental era.

In response to Baudrillard's animistic view of the perversity of the object, might we not ask about the exercise of that freedom which shaped desires in a project of reason and order, whose final pathos is called postmodernity? We have thus traversed an empty space and time, which has to be filled, and we have liberated a subject, who has to attain himself by a manageable consciousness, constructed step by step, carefully, and without error, demonstrated like a theorem about disposable nature. The seduction of the object, invoked in the act of assenting to that freedom of appropriation and shaped by the way of conceptualizng reason, hid multiple fractures and presaged disenchantment. Basically, postmodernity represents a change in the evaluation of the discursive text that modernity wove itself.

Artistic experience clearly pointed to the impoverished dystopian time, but postmodern thinkers thematized the state of affairs in a discourse legitimating its inevitability. Modernity's basic logic became apparent. The inevitable result of what the subject thought, the final role of the object, was the pathos of externality. Dystopian devaluation appeared to discredit the values which sponsored modernity's project. Then, the subject, who is also living existence, becomes nothing, and wanders unprotected or falls back into individualism. Its horizon of meaning is shrunk by the evaluations contained in the image of the world furnished by the owners of the mass media. This is one of the ways in which central societies face a crisis today. The veils of a historical interpretation have fallen, one which dressed itself up as the only interpretation. Nevertheless, in Latin America the same crisis without precise coordinates, based on our own historical circumstance, simulates a qualitative leap in the appropriation of a new destiny.

3. Transvestite Logic, or about Sexuality without Sex

m. The rebirth of a pristine reason in dialogue with the subject (Touraine)[17] or its restoration by European "insight, energy, courage of vision" (Habermas)[18] would not overcome the divorce between meaning-removed postmodern culture (actors or subjects) and instrumentality (society or social-Darwinist game rules). Meaning and instrumentality spring from the same exercise of signification by a mode of freedom, freedom of appropriation. The ontological horizon opened by modernity contained the first fruits of a rationalization which would end by devouring the aspirations of the subject. Baudrillard is clear here: the object's destiny exceeds the interpretations that can be made about it.[19]

n. Unfortunately, both Habermas's and Touraine's concerns are inspired by the idea of universal reason which still pretends to be preserved from any original sin. The modern dystopia, that is to say, postmodernity, is indeed "the self-inflicted destiny"[20] of modern European Reason's utopian effort. Habermas is wrong in viewing this as a mere historical error. As contemporary practice and social thought shows, modernity's normative content, accumulated in rationalized life-worlds, may give rise to more and more complex and competitive systems and legitimate the real conduct of social and economic actors. This does not deny that Habermas may be correct in saying that we find here "one of those false clichés in which systematic compulsion is condensed." Therefore, it is also false that "humanity is breaking off its alliance with nature and reverting to savagery just when it thought it had been freed from all constraints and was in control of its own destiny," as Touraine suggests.[21] In modernity the objectification of the freedom of appropriation through its other face, the will to domination, has already deliberately broken this alliance. Could there be a genuine alliance between the decider and what is perceived as a mere matter for decision? There is no surprise there. This is the western paradigm which continues to orient our mode of relating to nature.

A real change of paradigm would imply accepting the challenge to resignify the world from the viewpoint of *freedom to be* which would open the ontological horizon to development of consistent power, the power to be (not to have). The nature of freedom exercised in this way would permit us to construct the environment of a space lived as a habitat, not as the object of conquest of the subject's identity, which is precisely the rationale of freedom which inspires the postindustrial scientific, technological complex as well as the postmodern simulation narrative which legitimates it.

o. However, although their internal logic links modern optimism with postmodern pessimism, the manifestation of the latter sociocultural phenomenon is undergoing an inflection which justifies the concern and apprehension of thinkers like Touraine or Habermas.

The power of modernity's metanarratives resided in a compromise signified by the construction of a new society in the perspective of rational progress and ultimately human freedom. (Reason and freedom were sustained and at the same time realigned by the belief in the universal validity of the concept of man which suppresses differences or only acknowledges imperfect mirror images, always the shadows or contingencies of autonomous man and modern culture.) Nevertheless, modernity still had a limit in guilt. It could not accept the implications of its *Weltanschauung* without recurring to a legitimation based on a strong narrative. Therefore, it shaped a vision of the world and a manner of transforming it that had to morally involve the mentors, the protagonist, and the society custodian of that ideal of humanity in a common project. The discourse was principally directed to *us* Europeans. Postmodern discourse continues to speak as that same *we*, "the societies with which we are concerned," "the most highly developed societies,"[22] the societies where our scientific, technological apparatus has revealed the potentiality of instrumental reason and which, furthermore, remain under the self-imposed shelter of other peoples' consciousness of leadership. But unlike the other discourse which inspired the postmodern critical narrative, it prefers to express itself as the absence of narrative, because it has perfected its compromise with the idea of modernity. It has taken the other direction on the path of the limitations of moral duties and narrative justifications, adopting "strategies of the object." It has perfected a compromise with what is most characteristic in that instrumental reason present at its birth. What can be more characteristic of instrumental reason than *operativeness*, the best action (efficacy and efficiency) in achievement of objectives.

p. Heidegger correctly said that the essence of the technical is not technical. The essence of the technical is to be sought in what Gadamer calls "our prior decisions." For me that would be the act constituting the world. This constituent act actualizes freedom, qua capacity of signification. By it we configure a world, an order, a symbolic universe which makes the contingent segment of inevitable existence that we are, into a project of life.[23]

Nietzsche can be interpreted from this perspective. His critique uncovers the nihilism which leads to acceptance of a world referred to externality, determined by the object (although the subject imagines that it constructs it). Consequently, a plausible response to the dissociation between meaning and instrumentality ought to be sought in what is posited in the choice of meaning, in the ontological horizon opened in the act of constituting the world. Then I could not consistently discover instrumentality dissociated from meaning. It was always there contained in the exercise of that liberty of signification. What other manifestation could I expect? Besides, the problem of dissociation whether in these or other equivalent terms like identity and difference, public and private, only becomes a question from a perspective of meaning that does not contain it, which is precisely not the case of modernity's project. Postmodernity does not bring the problem to light because of a critical ambition; rather there is a general coincidence. Nor does it attempt to construct the history of humanity differently. It is simply that postmodernity harvests the dreams of modernity; it is the dystopia of modernity's utopian project. The complete submission of the *other* (peoples, men, and nature, conceived according to the old scheme of anthropocentric dissociation as *them*) takes the concrete form of the freedom of appropriation, the power of domination; it engendered the space of the free play of seduction where we find ourselves, that is, it set up the world as artifice, as implement exhausted in the occasion of use (and abuse). In reality, the game of seduction only ends by revealing itself in the vacuum of consumerist enjoyment. It can be stopped only at the cost of being unmasked.

q. So why should we be surprised that the real evaporates? Is it not strictly consistent that things flow toward their finish in a medium of constant absorption of psychological time? Is it not appropriate that interiority closes with the satisfaction of individual desires stimulated by publicity, celebrity magazines, the electronic newspaper, or the fantasy of interaction with the mass media? Baudrillard is right in saying that seduction takes control of all production and ends by annihilating it.[24] But this occurs only in a way analogous to how modifications of value during the life cycle of a product force the acceleration of continual innovations in the process of innovation to satisfy demands that explode geometrically. They deal the cards for a new departure from which the real (the empire of technology and cybernetic knowledge) can circulate, fascinating us, yet hiding themselves as project. Pure seduction, simulacrum, is a movement which shortens distances until it manages to confuse and dull thought and impede personal contacts—the encounter—through simultaneity of a crowd of fragmented signs with a clear goal of trapping us in the artificial net of its game.

Properly speaking, the teleological component of seduction is to be sought in the metanarrative which imposes a future, irreversible global society of information.[25] Paradoxically, seduction functionalizes[26] the logic of production. Better acting, that ideal of operative rationality, purports not only to satisfy our material lives, but it also postulates human self-realization, temporal values. It eliminates any classical rough ontological edges from modernity's old, secularized concept of the development of autonomous reason and radicalizes its instrumental character. The ultrametaphysical jokes of weak ontology, which Vattimo[27] attributes to postmodern thought, are found, I believe, in this transvestism as model of social practice, the unrestricted right to individual freedom of canned pleasure served to order, which exonerates humans from permanent personal engagements and from the anguish of meaning; it substitutes for the existential weight of local narratives of nonhegemonic societies, a new onto-teleological certainty of the technological object's logical necessity. The historical subjects which compute the multiplicity of narratives and in the last analysis of possible language games are obviously postindustrial societies. Once again power circulates in the same direction, even if it satisfies Foucault's wish that it do so without disciplinary compulsion.[28] The users have internalized it. They have been assimilated to computerized social organization.

One of the most detailed expressions of this project is the new alliance proposed by Yoneji Masuda's *Computopia*. Its ultimate goal is the "renaissance of teleological synergism" between man and the "Supreme Being," that is, Nature-God," *pace* Comte. In his scientistic optimism, the Japanese futurologist gives this the odd label of "the last living force."[29]

By Way of Conclusion

The ingenious play of words in the Italian refrain *dalle stelle alle stalle*[30] synthesizes our era's state of soul. Only a sigh, an instant, separates fascination from disenchantment. Or it does so whenever life is conceived only as a succession of expectations without permanence. Replacing Yahve by the golden calf or a welfare society where happiness rests on the possession of the latest computer chips does not suppress the ambiguity of the tension of the finite and infinite in our existence. Asking for meaning still awaits a response, whether in the words of Plato or in the exultation of the most frivolous television personality. The text of human life always demands legitimating discourse. Metaphysical questions stay with us even if we give them other names or propose their obsolescence. It would be impossible to live standing up if we make the axiological kaleidoscope our great simulated narrative. The planetary expansion of telecommunication and cybernetic systems does not guarantee communication. The information society is not necessarily the communication society. If knowledge is operative information, and the future of mankind is configured on this conceptual restriction, we are lost. The absence of thought hides existential interrogatives through an overdose of synergy in the narrative administration of technological sedatives with Dionysian stimulants. Real ecology is in the soul, or in unaccustomed and contaminated words, education in the assent to life, which involves awareness of our ontological and psychosocial limitation, the exercise of the freedom to resignify the world, and above all being consistent with that choice. One who holds both a club and marked cards can imagine that life is a game of chance in which irony is the only rule and where nothing has meaning. The game acquires a different drama, when we wager our hope of being, not of participating in historical destiny. Liberty is not systems software, optimally designed by some to be executed by others. When the imposition of freedom can enslave men more, then we cannot seriously discuss development, because the acknowledgment of the other is merely the result of application of ourselves.

The ontology of efficiency in dizzying individual hedonism and the exaltation of the image as postmodern metanarrative correspond to the abandonment of an axiology which limited the optimization of modern instrumental reason. The ambiguous structure of the new redesigned narrative facilitates dissociation in the system, and deepens the peripheral discourse of globalizing differences. Not everything is ephemeral. An irreversible march of technology is permanent Will man belong to the world of objects? Since objects will be invisible but omnipresent through a cybernetic network, they will be associated with him to connect him instantly to the artifices of his imagination and his desires.

Nevertheless, I believe that the sources of European thought conserve reflections for our time and specifically for this discussion. Consider the passage from the Protagoras:[31]

> And we must take care, my good friend, that the sophist in commending his wares, does not deceive us, as both merchant and dealer do in the case of our bodily food. For among the provisions, you know, in which these men deal, not only are they themselves ignorant of what is good or bad for the body, since in selling they commend them all, but the people who buy from them are so too, unless one happens to be a trainer or a doctor. And in the same way, those who take their doctrines the round of our cities, hawking them about to any odd purchaser who desires them, commend everything that they sell, and there may well be some of these too, my good sir, who are ignorant which of their wares is good or bad for the soul; and in just the same case are the people who buy from them, unless one happens to have a doctor's knowledge here also, but of the soul. So then, if you are well informed as to what is good or bad among these wares, it will be safe for you to buy doctrines from Protagoras or from anyone else you please: but if not, take care, my dear fellow that you do not risk your greatest treasure on a toss of the dice. For I tell you there is far more serious risk in the purchase of doctrines than in that of eatables.

Knowledge as understood and even more as practiced today in western civilization does not seem to be a sufficient alternative to permit postindustrial societies to emerge from the crisis of meaning which affects them, despite the operative efficacy of their scientific, technological apparatus. The crisis of meaning, we insist, is initially peculiar to these societies, not planetary. However, the anthropocentric temptation continues to inspire postures held by the members of the same family in this postmodern debate, even if with different nuances. That temptation will surely accentuate the crisis to unforeseen limits. When the sense of the existence of a people relies on progressive dependence on strategic demands to respond to its vocation to be in the world, it is because it has abandoned itself to the domination of objects. It has effectively entered the cycle of hysterisis. When individuals fall back into themselves or into communities of the like-minded, inflamed by pseudo-soteriological or gnostic slogans, they only exacerbate the threatening aspects of the crisis without confronting the implicit pathology of the results of the power of domination. The latter is the earthly legacy of modernity's freedom of appropriation, which produces the postmodern abscess at the heart of developed societies.

As Plato's text proclaims, wisdom would help us grow in our capacity to discriminate amid what the reality we must live offers and to broaden our comprehension of the sociocultural phenomenon which engages us. Gilles Lipovetsky has said that it is necessary "to avoid the catastrophic line of thought which intellectuals often lay out for us, all those who like to show that we are in a horrible universe without meaning or value, in a hell. [It is a matter of] simply thinking that this society is not exactly a paradise but neither is it a hell. That there are many resources, and that furthermore, it is not certain that we have no value."[32]

Consequently, I am convinced that Latin America has a great deal to offer in this crisis where postindustrial societies have lost their center, particularly to European consciousness. The contribution might be summed up in an image: extending our hands to have the opportunity to pass through the mirror. Perhaps thus we might find the courage to imagine a true Copernican revolution centered in the *other*.

Notes

1. It is worth observing that Habermas's challenge to postmodernity and his proposal to recuperate the program of emancipation is an implicit affirmation of postmodernity's derivation from the project of modernity. Without articulating a formal proof, I wish to note that there is an observable displacement in Habermas' sdiscourse, which obviously indirectly supports the argument set forth here. See especially his 1980 lecture on the occasion of receiving the Theodor Adorno Prize. See also *Der Philosophische Diskurs der Moderne* (Frankfurt am Main: Suhrkamp Verlag, 1985; Spanish translation: Buenos Aires: Taurus, 1989). I have consulted the translation that appeared in the journal *Punto de Vista*, 21 August 1984 (Buenos Aires), included in the useful collection *El debate Modernidad/Posmodernidad*, ed. Nicolás Casullo,(Buenos Aires: Ediciones El Cielo por Asalto, 1993) ,131-144.

2. Jean Baudrillard, *Seduction*, trans. Bruce Singer (New York: New World Perspectives, 1990), 13

3. Jean Baudrillard, *The Illusion of the End*, trans. Chris Turner (Stanford, Calif.: Stanford University Press, 1994), 116,

4. See H. Daniel Dei, *Discépolo: Todavía la esperanza* (Buenos Aires: Editorial Almagesto, Colección Perfiles, 1994). Commenting how he wrote another of his famous tangos, *Uno*, 1943, Discépolo tells us about the spiritual state in which he created: "That *neutral gear of the soul* is not a mere literary invention. . . . Perhaps the image 'if I had a heart' is savagely exaggerated [alluding to one of the lines of the tango] but one must live to understand it and live intensely, as so many live in my land and other lands. People suffer a great deal in our century. It is a terrible and precious period. . . . Just as a variable number changes the sum, the beautiful and tragic life of modern man is a game of delusion and of agonies which wear out hope . . . what we know . . . what we desire . . . what we love. There is nothing so horrendous as not believing, nor so sad, nor so profound. It is like the deep water of all dreams."

5. Jean Baudrillard, *The Illusion of the End*, 122.

6. An important element of my philosophical perspective is the distinction between *problem* and *question*.

> The critical, technical use of these notions allows us to dissolve and neutralize *at least* a great number, if not all, objections about the uselessness of philosophical answers. It allows us to discover the sense of philosophical investigation and overcome the perennial argument between deaf interlocutors about undesired consequences of their activity which are usually considered to be characteristic of philosophizing. The questions are interrogatives which open perspectives of sense to the one who poses them in their very formulation. . . . They light the way to comprehension of the world. They orient investigation and the search for truth, even if by their nature they are not positively resolved in the manner of scientific answers. What is clarified in the scientific answer is mediated by information and the instruments. In other words, what confronts us in a problem is an unknown which is removed only by a missing datum which may always appear in time. Therefore, we look for solutions from science. We seek to fill up present voids in information. Hence the confidence in its efficacy, even if the solution is far away. But it is fallacious to argue, as positivism does in contemporary culture, that *all* questions can and will be resolved by science in the near or remote future. Thus, some of our contemporaries believe that the problematic of human affairs can be made uniform because we are able to apply different methods and procedures to resolve problems in every sphere of social activity.

Cf. H. Daniel Dei, "El sentido de la indagación filosófica," 71-76 in *Revista de Filosofía de la Universidad de Costa Rica,* no. 63-64, vol. 26, 1968, 74.

7. Ludwig Wittgenstein, *Notebooks 1914-1916*, July 6, 1916, 74, ed. and trans. G. E. M. Anscombe (New York: Harper and Row, Torchbook edition, New York, 1969).

8. Cf. H. Daniel Dei, "La cuestión del hombre. Invitación al sentido de nuestra vida," in *Propuestas de Antropología Argentina III*, ed. C. E. Berbeglia (Buenos Aires: Editorial Biblos, 1994).

9. See Gilles Lipovetsky, *La era del vacío. Ensayos sobre el individualismo contemporáneo* (Barcelona:Anagrama, 1986).

10. The phrase echoes the title of a splendid novel by the Peruvian Ciro Alegría.

11. Jean Baudrillard, *The Illusion of the End*, 120.

12. Jean Baudrillard, *Fatal Strategies*, trans. Philip Beitchman and W. G. J. Niesluchowski, ed. Jim Fleming (Brooklyn: 1990, Barcelona: 1991, Semiotext(e)-Pluto) 181 and ff.

13. Cf. Hans-Georg Gadamer, *Truth and Method*, trans. Jack Weinsheimer and Donald G. Marshall (New York: Crossroad, second revised edition, 1989), 91-99.

14. Cf. Gianni Vattimo, *The Transparent Society*, trans. David Webb (Baltimore: Johns Hopkins University Press, 1992). See also *The End of Modernity. Nihilism and Hermeneutics in Postmodern Culture*, trans. and intro. by Jon R. Snyder (Baltimore: Johns Hopkins University Press, 1988).

15. Alain Touraine, *Critique of Modernity*, trans. David Macey (Oxford: Blackwell, 1995), 179, 198.

16. Tzvetan Todorov, *The Conquest of America: The Problem of the Other*, trans. Richard Howard (New York: Harper and Row, 1984), 5.

17. Alain Touraine, *Critique of Modernity*, 379.

18. Jürgen Habermas, *The Philosophical Discourse of Modernity*, 367 (and generally ch. 12, IV). Just as Christopher Columbus incarnated the redemption by reason, Habermas believes that this redemption can only be accomplished by Europe. But this pathos is not exclusive to him. The majority of European thinkers accompany him. Gadamer has clearly grasped this acritical side of European consciousness, 44, in *La herencia de Europa* (Barcelona: Editorial Península, 1990): ". . . even without wanting

to, we will have preconceptions and overlook the evidence of [other] cultures." On Christopher Columbus see *Los cuatro viajes del Almirante y su testamento*, Ed. y prologue by I. B. Anzoátegui (Mexico, Austral, 1984). Cf. R. A. Herra, "Descubrir o conquistar el Paraíso. Premodernidad modernidad, posmodernidad," in H. Daniel Dei, *Poder y libertad en la socieda postmoderna* (Buenos Aires: Almagesto, first edition, 1995, second edition, 1998).

19. Baudrillard, "In every period, in some form, the object . . . has exceeded all the interpretations made about it. But . . . even the modern, industrially manufactured produced object (about which it might be thought that exact interpretations could be given because of its artificial nature) in some way exceeds the interpretations. Not even the disenchanted, de-sacralized modern object is identified with its interpretation . . . a Japanese manufacturer would tell us that every object created by industry has an immanent divinity . . . the most humble objects still have a secret, even for the one who has manufactured them. That an object has been manufactured or produced does not mean that it is possessed, because that object follows its own destiny which we never know. " Cf "La implosión del pensamiento," interview with Jean Baudrillard by Sergio Cecchetto in *La Prensa*, Buenos Aires, Sunday, February 13, 1994.

20. Jürgen Habermas, *The Philosophical Discourse of Modernity*, 367.

21. Alain Touraine, *Critique of Modernity*, 372.

22. Jean-François Lyotard, *The Postmodern Condition*: *A Report on Knowledge*, trans. Geoff Bennington and Brian Massumi, foreword Frederick Jameson (Minneapolis: University of Minnesota Press, 1984, 1997), xxiii, 14.

23. H. Daniel Dei, "La cuestión del hombre."

24. Jean Baudrillard, *Seduction*, passim, especially, 47.

25. Compelling confirmation of this is the Information Network Systems (INS) scheme promoted by Nippon Telegraph and Telephone Public Corporation and Yoneiji Masuda's *La sociedad informatizada como sociedad post-industrial* (Madrid: Fundesco-Tecnos, 1984).

26. Functionalize" is used in the sense that Foucault asociates with the term "power."

27. The end of modernity in the last analysis.

28. "Curso del 14 de enero de 1976," in *Microfísica del Poder* (Madrid: Ediciones La Piqueta, 1980).

29. Yoneji Masuda, *La sociedad informatizada*, 176-177.

30. Literally, from the stars to the stables.

31. Plato, *Protagoras*, 313 c-e, W. R. M. Lamb trans. (Cambridge, Mass.: Loeb Library edition, Harvard University Press, 1957), 106-109.

32. Interview with Gilles Lipovetsky by María Luisa López reproduced from the Mexican newspaper *Jornada*, by the periodical *La Maga*, Buenos Aires, August 10, 1994.

Index

About the Author

H. Daniel Dei is Professor of Philosophy at the University of Morón in Argentina. He also lectures at the Graduate School of Business at Palermo University and the Open and Distance "Hernandarias" Foundation. Since 1998 he has been Visiting Professor at the University of Granada (Spain). He is Director of the Methodology, Epistemology, and Thesis Department at the University of Morón, and of the Institute of Research in the Philosophy Department at the University of Morón.

He is a former Professor at the Universities of Buenos Aires, Belgrano, CAECE, of (and at the Higher Formation Institutes of the Argentine State, and Visiting Professor at the Institute of Administration Sciences of the Catholic University of Córdoba, the Technological Foundation of Mar del Plata, the School of Law at National University of Rosario and the National University of Mar del Plata, and has been researcher and Visiting Professor at Universität Leipzig.

His published books include: *Recursos humanos en las organizaciones* (Docencia, 1995); *Poder y libertad en la sociedad posmoderna* (Almagesto, 1995, 1998); *Discépolo: todavía la esperanza* (RundiNuskín, 1990; Almagesto, 1995, 2000); *Antropodicea. La cuestión del hombre* (Almagesto, 1997); *Psicosociología de las organizaciones* (Docencia, 2002, co-editor); *Lógica de la Distopía. Fascinación, desencanto y libertad* (Docencia, 2002), *Pensar y hacer en investigación* (2 vols., Docencia, 2002, as editor); *Gestión con el Personal* (Docencia, 2002; 2003; coeditor).

About the Translator

James G. Colbert is a native of Boston, who is a Professor of Philosophy at Fitchburg State College. He has also taught at Boston State College and the University of Navarre in Pamplona, Spain. He is author or coauthor of five books: *La evolución de la lógica simbólica y sus implicaciones filosóficas* (Pamplona: E.U.N.S.A., 1968); *Curso de iniciación al marxismo: cuatro lecciones* [with Thomas J. Blakeley], (Pamplona: E.U.N.S.A., 1977); *Marxism and Alternatives* [with Thomas J. Blakeley, William Gavin, and Tom Rockmore], (Dordrecht, Holland: Reidel, 1981; *Philosophy and the Family, Their Values* [with Thomas J. Blakeley and Frank Soo], (Oneonta, N.Y: East-West Books, 1987); *Computing and Logic: Mathematics and Language* [with Thomas J. Blakeley and Glenn Satty], (München: Philosophia Verlag, 1988). He has also published numerous articles and reviews, especially in *Studies in Soviet Thought* and *Nuestro Tiempo*.

Dr. Colbert is also participating in the Vargas Ugarte project sponsored by the Pontificia Universidad Católica del Perú in Lima. Dr. Colbert has edited the transcription of José de Aguilar's *Metaphysica* and *De Ortu et Interitu,* and is working on his *Commentarium in Aristotelis De Anima*.